NINE PASSES

*Fly Fishing through
the Past and Present
of the High Sierra*

TODD BRUCE

Black Swift Press

Edited by Bri Bruce and Tyler Walicek
Cover design by JT Bruce
Cover images by Todd Bruce
Interior layout by Bri Bruce

Photo credit: From WATERS OF THE GOLDEN TROUT COUNTRY by Charles McDermand, copyright 1946 by Charles McDermand. Used by permission of G. P. Putnam's Sons, a division of Penguin Group (USA) LLC.

Photo of Charles McDermand courtesy San Francisco Labor Local 1100 Report, January 13, 1967.

Published by Black Swift Press

Visit www.ninepasses.com for more information.

FOREWORD

Todd Bruce's *Nine Passes* is about two subjects: family and fly fishing. It is also about how these two elements are inextricably intertwined in our family's history and weave a three-quarter century tale of fly fishing in the High Sierra. This is a story of a single five-week backpacking trip, the purpose of which was to fish many of the same places that our family visited and fished, from the 1940s to present day, all the while retracing the steps of a cultish book written in the 1940s by a High Sierra fly fishing legend.

I can also tell you what this book is *not* about. In this age of over-achieving athletic one-upmanship, this is not a tale of who can hike the farthest, complete the John Muir Trail the fastest, backpack with the least amount of gear, or catch the biggest trout. It is a reconnection to the wonders of fly fishing in the High Sierra and a deep appreciation for those that went before us to document and preserve an environment in Western North America that is completely unique.

As a part of the family, I want to share some insights that will hopefully set the stage for Todd's story. To understand the nature of this book, it is first necessary to provide a bit of background into the history of the Bruce Clan. There were four of us "kids:" myself, Eric, Todd, and Tammi, the youngest. We grew up in the East San Francisco Bay Area, and our family vacation every year was backpacking somewhere in the Sierra, Trinity Alps, or Marble Mountains. Growing up in the 60s, it was all we knew and it was the only vacation we ever wanted as kids. Our parents, Wayne and Barbara, had grown up in the outdoors, something they, too, learned from their respective families.

Our family had the incredible good fortune of growing up in a time and place in California that was without significant social ills and enabled a childhood filled with the opportunity to roam free, to be outside and appreciate the outdoors, and most importantly to develop a deeply ingrained attraction to fly fishing. Todd came by that attraction through his family ties as well as through his upbringing in California. For Todd, it is both a story of nature, as well as nurture, that fly fishing has become such a significant part of his life.

To say that Todd was born with a fly rod in hand is not too far from the truth. All of us Bruce kids first learned to fish with a fly rod. For Todd and I, backpacking was the means to the ends—a way to get up to the great High Sierra trout streams, rivers, and lakes. The family attraction to the out-of-doors came on both sides. Our mother came from a family with a rich tradition of horse packing in the southern Sierra Nevada backcountry. Our maternal great-grandfather, George R. Goldman, owned a large ranch in the central valley of California and used to take our mother with him on his trips to the high country.

Another aspect of our childhood that played a key role in developing our love of the outdoors was scouting. Todd was an Eagle Scout, the third one in his family. Our father was an Eagle Scout, and his father before him was his Scoutmaster, just as our father was our Scoutmaster. We participated in scouting in an age of unfettered freedom from lawsuits, and from political correctness run amok. We learned about leadership and conservation, and how to be completely self-reliant in venturing outdoors. We were lucky that our troop also had a high backpacking ethic, and that we also took a weeklong backpacking trip each summer with the Scouts. Many of our family backpack routes intersected with the areas we visited with Troop 236 from Danville, California.

The genesis of Todd's trip actually traces back to a single unassuming book. There were a few books about the Sierra and backpacking that I remember from our family bookcase growing up in California, but I never really paid too much attention to them as a kid. Our parents absorbed them and passed on the knowledge to us through "on-the-job-training" during our family vacations. One book that I do remember was *Starr's Guide to the Sierras* by Walter A. Starr, Jr., originally published in 1934. Starr was an early member of the Sierra Club, and the book was a valuable source of information on the Sierra hiking routes that we used for planning our family trips.

As important as the ranch was to our mother and her family, by the time our great-grandfather passed away, there was not much of a legacy left to pass down to the family. "The Ranch," as it was always referred to by our mother's family, was sold in 1955 after George R. Goldman passed away the year before. All that managed to survive the next three generations were a few scrapbooks, a lot of family stories, and one small treasure of a book with an inscription written by a man named Les to my maternal grandfather, George R. Goldman, on the inside jacket cover. This very innocuous little book was titled *Waters of the Golden Trout Country* and was written by a gentleman named Charles "Mac" McDermand. I remember it, but know that I never read it. It was a boring-looking book for a young kid.

Waters of the Golden Trout Country is a small hardbound book with a blue cloth cover that contains 162 pages with a few black and white photographs in it. After my mother passed away, I happened to end up with the book that was amassed with a few of my mother's possessions. Several years later, after yet another move in my Navy career (where I seemed to keep moving the same old stuff from duty station to duty station) I was cleaning out boxes of random items. I came across Mac's book, and ended up leafing through it, noticing first the inscription, and then realizing that I had found a family gem.

Waters of the Golden Trout Country chronicles Mac's journeys over three separate trips during two summers in the 1940s as he trekked throughout the High Sierra, fly fishing in as many locations as possible and documenting the fish he caught. As I carefully absorbed it, I realized that we had visited many of the places he wrote about. I became infatuated with the book and passed it on to Todd. The rest, as the saying goes, is history. Todd longed to recreate Mac's journey. I will let him share the reasons why.

Todd completed this 300-mile-long trek as a tribute to Mac, and to those who have helped to preserve the High Sierra. Mostly, it is a tribute to our parents for imbuing in us a life-long appreciation of fly fishing in the High Sierra.

Finally, I am deeply honored that Todd let me and my son, Nicholas, join him for a week of his adventure, and that he asked me to write the foreword for *Nine Passes*. I hope that Todd's story will inspire you to take a moment to consider the truly important things in your life, and motivate you to make lifetime memories of your own. Good reading!

Scott Bruce
January 19, 2015

ACKNOWLEDGEMENTS

First, I would like to thank my wonderful and lovely wife Heidi for her understanding, support, and facilitation efforts for this trip. You were always there to support me through the months of planning and my preoccupation with my gear, logistical quandaries, and content additions. Thank you so very much for being there for me in spite of all the time it took me away from you. It, too, was a long journey for you. I love you so very much.

A special thanks goes to my eldest brother, Scott and his son, Nicholas. They took time out from their busy lifes to fly across the country to join me on part of this trek. Your passion for fishing, the mountains and backpacking rivals that of mine. Thank you, Scott, for providing the foreward for this book.

I certainly can't forget my son, Justin "JT," and daughter, Brianna "Bri." Thanks for letting me share my love of the outdoors, the Sierra Nevada in particular, with you. I dragged you along on so many trips and I think you both understand me better than most. You both have been integral components of this project. The editing and production efforts by Bri were extensive and it has brought us even closer together. Without your vision, creativity, and drive, this book would not be what it is today. JT's talent and creativity with the cartagraphy and graphics is endless and without equal. I can always count on you. Thanks, I love you both.

Tyler Walicek spent many hours editing my manuscript and deserves a special thanks for his talents and suggestions.

Last and not least, a special thanks goes to Mac for writing a special book that inspired me, energized me, and helped give me a purpose for this trek.

INTRODUCTION

In August of 1945, a citrus rancher from Orosi in Tulare County, California, gathered a group of friends and family for a horse pack trip to fish the Kern River area of the Sierra Nevada. His name was George R. Goldman. Although he had made this kind of trip before, on this particularly special trip he had invited his eleven-year-old granddaughter, Barbara. She was tough and well accustomed to the outdoors, having spent her summers growing up on a ranch learning how to cook, work in the fruit packing sheds, ride horses, fish, and even shoot a gun.

The rest of the group included George's brother, Edward A. Goldman, his niece, Helen Goldman, an assortment of friends, and the horse packers that George hired. They left from the Horse Corral Meadows Pack Station in the Sequoia National Forest, east of Visalia, packing on horseback to the mighty Kern River for an opportunity to fish and enjoy the wilderness of the High Sierra.

The trail was long and dusty as it meandered through some of the most beautiful High Sierra scenery, including Rowell and Sugarloaf Meadows, Roaring River, Cloud Canyon, alongside the magnificent knife-like ridge called the Whaleback, and Colby Lake. Eventually the trail climbed over Colby Pass at an elevation of 12,250 feet above sea level. "Goldman Camp" was established next to the Kern River and it was the Gilbert rainbow trout, native to that river, and the golden trout, native to its tributaries, that was their quarry.

This pack trip and fishing expedition was Barbara's first exposure to this part of the Sierra Nevada, a springboard for a lifetime of fishing, backpacking, and many opportunities to share such a magical place with friends and family for many years to come.

When Barbara passed away in 1989, one of her prized possessions ended up in the hands of her eldest son, Scott—my brother. It was a book written by avid outdoorsman and fly fisherman Charles K. McDermand titled *The Waters of the Golden Trout Country*. The book was a gift to George R. Goldman, my great-grandfather, from a man named Les. After reading it several times, Scott shared this piece of treasure with me. Charles McDermand's stories of fly fishing and backpacking immediately tugged at something deeply rooted within me. I read it, then reread it several times so as not to miss a single fishing experience painted by the author. He was a true artist and had an amazing way of telling a story and sharing his experiences that continued to fuel a burning fire in me. It was this fire that sparked the motive to plan a trek that took many years to finally execute.

My parents grew up in different parts of California doing very much the same things: hiking, fishing, hunting, backpacking, and enjoying the outdoors. They shared that mutual interest and passion with their children. I started fishing when I was four years old, where my first recollection of fishing was with a fly. And, no pun intended, I was hooked.

As a kid, I took hold of every opportunity to fish the local waters around the small town of Alamo, California, where I grew up, the foothills of Mt. Diablo at my disposal. I would ride my bicycle down to the creek and fish for bluegill, crayfish, and suckerfish. I experimented with bait (usually cheese, bologna, or salmon eggs) and a variety of flies, and sometimes all it took was a bare hook. My brothers and I would spend days hiking and fishing all the stock ponds for bass and bluegill. We had thousands of acres of cattle land that we considered our backyard. My best success came with a balsa wood fly that I tied to look like an adult dragonfly. I took many big bass from those ponds.

However, it was the Sierra trout and a dry fly that became

my true passion. Fly fishing for sierra trout, for me, offered an escape and a sense of freedom. Being on the water and in the woods was comfortable, and I always found peace and adventure there. Not many summers would pass without some sort of trip into the Sierra.

Retiring after a thirty-two-year career as a firefighter finally gave me the opportunity to set out on an extended journey. My goals for this adventure were threefold. First, I wanted to fish the rivers, streams, and lakes that Charles McDermand (or "Mac" as he was called by his fishing friends) wrote about in his book, *The Waters of the Golden Trout Country*. I wanted to do in one backpacking trip what Mac did in three trips over the course of two summers. Secondly, I wanted to revisit the waters and areas where I had been as a kid. I have many fond memories of fishing and backpacking the High Sierra and wanted to repeat them before I loose them. Lastly, I have been very interested in studying the changes that have occurred over the years. Mac provides a strong account of the quality of the fisheries within the High Sierra during his era. He found "lunker" fish to three feet long, "steelheads" in Lake Italy and Dragon Lake, eighteen-inch golden trout, as well as fishless waters. My great-grandfather had huge success with the Gilbert rainbows of the Kern River and with the golden trout of its tributaries. Most importantly, I wanted to answer the following question: What is the fishing like today compared to seventy years ago? Along the way, I also attempted to look at what other changes have occurred in the High Sierra.

In the summer of 2012, I left Tuolumne Meadows on August 12th. Intent on keeping my goals at the forefront, I was excited to be back in the wilderness with my fly rod. With only two food drops and mostly hiking solo, I climbed up and over nine major passes along the crest of the Sierra Nevada. The highest pass was Forester Pass at 13,180 feet above sea level. I finally walked out of the wilderness on September 15th after trekking over 300 miles, fishing countless bodies of water, large and small, and weighing thirty pounds lighter.

This book is dedicated to my mother and father, Barbara and Wayne. They started it all by planting the seed and they kept the passion of the wilderness alive inside me. I miss you, Mom, and thanks for being there with me on part of this trek, Dad.

6/19/46

To George R. Goldman

*I am sure this will bring to mind the whole
tantalizing atmosphere of the "High Sierra."*

Regards,

Les

FLY FISHING THE HIGH SIERRAS

No more can I imagine
the impossible stillness
of the lake at dawn,
than I can see the arc of your line
above the water.

You work a fly along the shores
stepping between granite boulders,
the High Sierra frost of dawn
in your bones.

Almost, I can hear the whir of your leader,
the tick of your reel,
a fin work at the water's surface.

Later, you will sit warming by a fire
stoked by fallen pine,
the hiss of sap a symphony at dusk.

Tonight you will dream
of the fish you've pulled up
from the blue depths, wrestled ashore,
and in the tenfold silence that follows,
glimpse the clarity of the stars
in the seamless night.

- B.L.Bruce
excerpt from *The Weight of Snow*

The Author at Rose Lake

NINE PASSES

*Fly Fishing through
the Past and Present
of the High Sierra*

TODD BRUCE

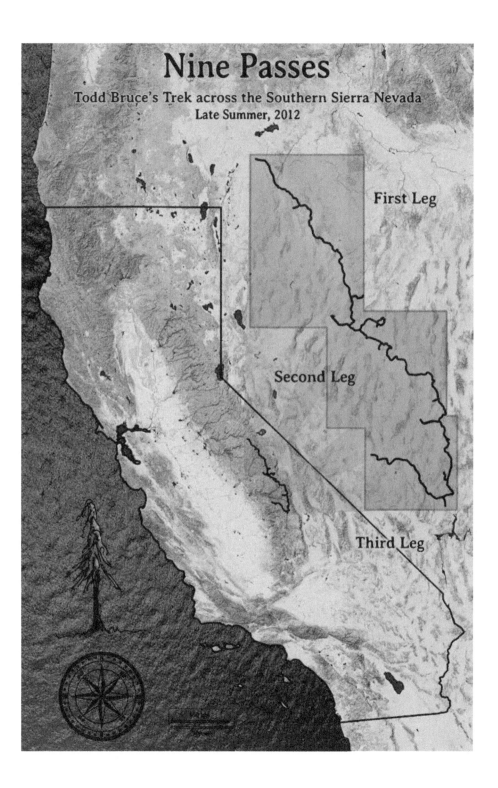

Nine Passes

Todd Bruce's Trek across the Southern Sierra Nevada
Late Summer, 2012

First Leg

Second Leg

Third Leg

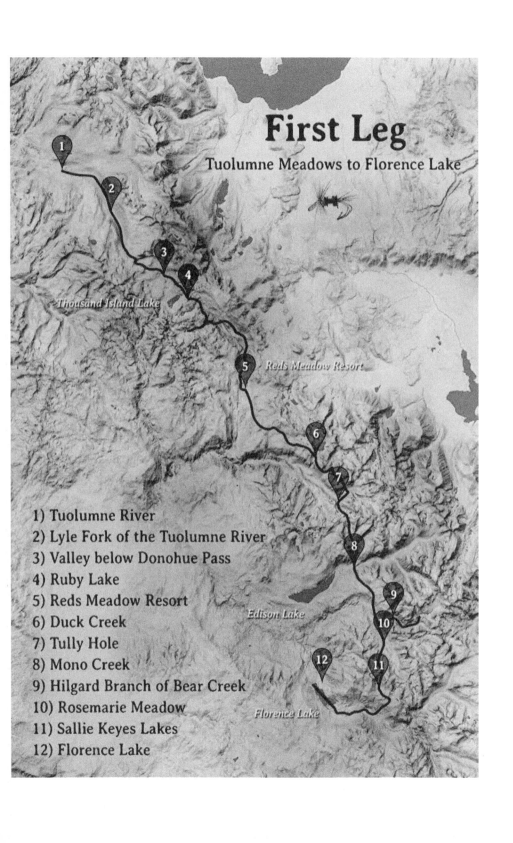

First Leg
Tuolumne Meadows to Florence Lake

1) Tuolumne River
2) Lyle Fork of the Tuolumne River
3) Valley below Donohue Pass
4) Ruby Lake
5) Reds Meadow Resort
6) Duck Creek
7) Tully Hole
8) Mono Creek
9) Hilgard Branch of Bear Creek
10) Rosemarie Meadow
11) Sallie Keyes Lakes
12) Florence Lake

Thousand Island Lake

Reds Meadow Resort

Edison Lake

Florence Lake

CHAPTER 1

The Start of a Fishing Journey

Tuolumne Meadows to Reds Meadow

"This one is all yours, Todd," my father told me as we all sat on the bank of Sugarloaf Creek for a quick lunch. Dad was referring to the small, solitary trout swimming about in the pool just below the trail crossing. I had eyed that pool the second we arrived. The year was 1967, and I was on a backpacking trip with my parents, my two brothers, and my younger sister. We had just been packed in on horseback from the Horse Corral Pack Station in the Sequoia National Forest. The packer and his stock having just left us, Mom and Dad busied themselves, getting all our gear rearranged and readied to hit the trail. Lunch was first on our agenda.

While Mom was getting lunch ready, I rigged my fly rod and tied on a fly from my fly box. I was fighting back a rush of jitters from the excitement. At age six, I was still learning to fly fish. My parents taught my siblings and me to first fish with a fly. We learned to rig a proper fly rod, and then we learned how to tie the flies to the leader using the modified cinch knot. Before we were allowed to cast a fly, we were encouraged to "dabble," as my parents called it. This technique is simple and requires the angler to dangle the fly over the water and make it dance on the water's surface, the way that an insect might. Aside from dabbling, we were also shown how to swing the fly to the top of a riffle and let it drift downstream. A traditional cast would come later.

I approached the pool cautiously, all while keeping a fixed gaze on the fish in the clear water. Creeping on all fours, moving stealthily like a lion stalking its prey, I moved to a position behind a small willow bush. I carefully removed my fly from the cork handle of my rod and patiently sat there dabbling my fly over and around the fish. I sat there for what seemed an eternity, chasing the fish around the pool with my fly. "The fish can see red and it scares them," Dad eventually told me. I was wearing a red shirt. He suggested that I change, so I retreated to my pack and dug deep to pull out a different colored shirt. I figured a black shirt would do just fine.

The author, age six, at Sugarloaf Creek

Back at the pool, the fish didn't seem to notice my fly, and I was thinking I might need to change flies. Then it happened. The fish made a quick dash in the direction of my fly and with one splashing leap he was hooked. I hauled him in and proudly stood next to the creek for a few pictures. From that point on, I never wore a red shirt when I fished.

The author, wearing black, at Sugarloaf Creek

* * *

In the two or three days leading up to my trip, I had butterflies in my stomach, awaiting my departure. Feeling both unsettled and fired up, my thoughts were constantly fixed on my gear, food list, emergency backup plans, and how much I would miss my family. All the time, thought, and energy that went into getting ready for the journey were beginning to boil, and I needed relief. I needed to get into the Sierra.

My wife, Heidi, her daughter, Jade, son, Jasper, and Simon, Jade's boyfriend, wanted to spend the first couple of days with me and send me off with a proper *bon voyage*! They planned to hike in the first day and spend the night with me before I set off into the wilderness for the next four to five weeks.

* * *

The drive to and then through Yosemite National Park is always a spectacular one. The smell of the pine trees, the granite monoliths, and the thousands of tourists all are part of the excitement. We passed a massive buck deer in the meadow alongside the road, lying still as a statue, completely unafraid. He seemed to know the park is a safe place to be, a place where hunters cannot get to him.

We arrived at Tuolumne Meadows Campground and were discouraged to find it full. After driving around, we found an empty campsite and decided to claim it after talking to the neighbor. His name was Jim (a sheriff's deputy for Los Angeles County), and he told us that the occupant of the site had paid for the night but decided to leave early because of the rain earlier in the day.

We settled in, had a dinner of freeze-dried chicken with rice, and laid out our ground cloth and sleeping bags. At about two in the morning, we woke to drops of rain from a passing storm and piled into the camper on the back of the truck to attempt to sleep the rest of the morning undisturbed.

We awoke the next morning to clear blue skies without a single cloud. Making our morning coffee and breakfast and taking a few pictures consumed the morning hours before we packed our backpacks. I kept a keen eye on the section of river just down from our campsite where a few kids were wading about, attempting to fish. I had to hold back my desire to explore it so we could get on our way in a timely fashion.

Fishing always seems to be the first thing on my mind when out in the woods. As a kid, I would size up the nearest creek or lake when we arrived at camp or when we hiked along the trail. That is how I felt that morning. While drinking my coffee, I quietly thanked Mom and Dad for teaching me how to fly fish—although catching trees and bushes in the process was my specialty, more so back then than it is today. It was a struggle to not rig up my rod and cast a fly on that section of the Tuolumne River near the campsite.

Tuolumne Meadows Campground send-off party

The last time I was in Tuolumne Meadows was in 1971, when I backpacked with my family to Vogelsang. We hiked up into the Vogelsang area hoping for some great fishing and to visit a part of the Yosemite high country that none of us had seen before. After a few days of hiking to get up to the lakes, we were overwhelmed with several days of heavy rain, thunder, and hail. We all tried to make the best of the situation and fish as much as we could, but the weather got the best of us. Soaked to the bone, and not able to dry out our gear, we gave up and packed out. It was a short trip, with lousy fishing, that left us wretched. Oddly, we never went back to the Vogelsang area.

Tuolumne Meadows to Vogelsang, 1971

By 10:00 a.m. we were on the trail. A few clouds quickly moved in overhead as we hiked the trail along the Lyell Fork of the Tuolumne River, a wide, picturesque canyon with granite peaks on all sides. When the first raindrops started to fall, Heidi asked, "Should we put our raingear on?" I confidently replied, "No," as I explained that I didn't think we would get hit hard with rain anytime too soon.

Three minutes later, it began to pour. Thunder clapped all around us as we ran for cover under a small grove of lodgepole pine. It wasn't long before it began to hail. We pulled out our tarps and ate a lunch of cheese, avocado, and salami on tortillas.

* * *

We arrived at Ireland Creek by mid-afternoon and found a flat area to camp across the river from the trail. While dodging the raindrops between bouts of thunder, we made camp, pitching a tarp between two trees. While we were out collecting firewood around the camp, we came across a porcupine. They are surprisingly clumsy and slow while on the ground. We followed him at a safe distance as he scurried about in an attempt to escape. When we returned to camp, I enjoyed watching Simon attempt to start a fire with wet wood and a flint and steel. He eventually gave up and got a fire going using the lighter.

The rain sprinkled on and off throughout the afternoon. I fished a few holes of the Lyell Fork before it began to rain too hard. The only fish I was able to coax to my flies were a few small six-inch brook trout. We spent the rest of the afternoon sitting around beneath the tarp. Jade and Simon played guitar and sang songs while Heidi played a card game of Rummy with Jasper, beating him eighty-five points to negative sixty-five points. Jasper gave up!

I awoke early the next morning to the sounds of the river. As I lay in my sleeping bag, it seemed that the river's rambling was louder than it had been the night before. The air was damp and cool as I emerged from my cozy down bag, and I had a good fire going and water boiling in no time. I wandered over to the river's edge with a cup of mocha to find that the water level had risen considerably overnight. The water was a little murky, too.

It was apparent that the upper reaches of the Lyell Fork Canyon had seen a lot of rain.

After the others got up, we broke camp, forded the river, and found a place to stash everyone else's packs. They were going to hike with me for a while, and then turn around and head back to the truck after lunch. About a mile and a half from camp, we stopped at a nice pool on a bend in the river to fish and eat lunch. It was warm, and the sun occasionally broke through the clouds as we sat on the grassy banks of the river.

Heidi, Jasper, Simon, and I all caught fish on that stretch of river. I was using a yellow-bodied, brown-hackled Stimulator and landed many small fish, but none of them were larger than six inches. All of the fish seemed to be some type of hybrid between brook and golden trout. One small fellow had the well-defined parr mark features of a golden trout and the red dots of the brook trout.

Mac caught his first golden trout in 1934. He used a number twelve Silver Doctor fly, and the joy of that experience stayed with him for many years. It was this very same section of river where Mac started his journey. When he set out in 1944, his goal was to prospect every major lake and stream in the Sierra Nevada for trout to find where the golden trout lived. Because the John Muir Trail passed dozens of lakes and crossed rivers and streams that were untouched by roads, this section of the Sierra Nevada seemed ideal for Mac to use as a starting point. The relatively new John Muir Trail was the perfect route for his exploration, as it stretched almost 200 miles through the central Sierra range and provided access to most of the golden trout waters.

Mac backpacked solo on his trip in July of 1944. He fished with a seven-foot fly rod, using a 3X tapered leader made of cat gut. In this section of river, he used Royal Coachman, black gnats, and yellow-bodied Gray Hackle flies to catch Eastern brook, Loch Leven, and rainbow trout up to twelve inches.

Mac talks a lot about the Loch Leven trout that he caught during his time in the High Sierra. Often, the fish were big, feisty, and put up a grand fight. I remember the name being used as a kid, but never really put it all into context back then. Loch Leven and brown trout are one and the same. Now, the term "Loch Leven" is no longer used here in the Sierra and is considered an outdated term that has since faded away.

In 1885, the first brown trout were brought to America from Germany. They were called German brown trout, or Van Behr trout, after the member of the German Fisheries Society that sent them over. In 1894, North American lakes were stocked with brown trout from Loch Leven, Scotland. The lakes in that region of Scotland were simply named Loch One, Loch Two, etc. Loch Leven is the eleventh lake in the chain, thus the name Loch Leven.

The trout from the two regions were the same species of trout; however, due to the differences in food supply, mineral content of the water, and life cycles, the fish had a slightly different appearance. The Loch Leven fish had a somewhat silvery coat, with slight differences in spots and darkness, and one seemed to be heavier than the other. Some anglers insisted that there was a difference and that they could distinguish one from the other.

In Scotland and Germany, the brown trout either stays at home in one lake or river system, or is a sea-run migratory fish. A 1957 booklet on the trout of California presented by the State of California Department of Fish and Game says that the "sea-run" browns returning from the ocean are quite silvery, resembling steelhead, and may lack the red spots. The brown trout have been found to be too expensive and too cannibalistic to raise in captivity under their hatchery program.

According to the California Department of Fish and Game, the offspring of the original stocks from Germany and Scotland were crossing in the wild and were becoming mixed in the state hatcheries. Thus, in the early 1930s, the two sub-species were declared synonymous, and brown trout (*Salmo trutta*) was made the official name. However, during the 1930s and 1940s, Loch Leven was still a popular name for the brown trout in the Sierra.

It was just after noon when the clouds started to close in on us. I was anxious to get on the trail and over Donohue Pass so I could begin my own odyssey. It looked like rain was soon to follow, and my goal was to camp at Rush Creek for the night. Within ten minutes of saying goodbye to my family in the meadow next to the river, it started to rain, continuing off and on until I got to the Lyell Fork Bridge.

View halfway up to Donohue Pass

Stopping to fish at the bridge, I met another hiker from Sun River, Oregon, named Kevin. He was eating peanut butter out of a big jar. I thought it unusual that someone would bring so much peanut butter—and the jar, too. We chatted for a while as a small group of backpackers descended into the area to look for a campsite. Suddenly, the quiet and tranquil little glen we were in was bustling with chatter. It continued to rain off and on as the other hikers scoured the area for a campsite. I fished the creek with a red-bodied Royal Humpy and caught more small hybrids before feeling the need to push onward.

The rain fell harder and harder as I pushed up the hill toward Donohue Pass. Nearly soaked to the bone, I had to stop and pitch the tarp at the vacant trail crew camp just below the pass. Once the tarp was up, I changed into dry clothes, ate freeze-dried beef stroganoff for an early dinner, and attempted to take a nap, hoping the rain would let up a little.

Donohue Pass

It was six o'clock when the rain finally stopped. I made a last minute decision to summit the pass. The trail felt like one long set of stairs, and I aptly named them the Donohue Stairs. I made it to the top with an hour or so of sunlight left. The pass, at an elevation of 11,056 feet, was shrouded in clouds, and I was disappointed that I didn't have a view of the valley below. I caught glimpses of the valley the entire way up, and I was hoping to get a good picture once I reached the top. No such luck. I was left with sore muscles and the threat of more rain.

When Mac arrived at the summit of Donohue Pass, he, too, was stiff and sore. We were both carrying heavy packs, and I wondered if I had done well by meticulously planning and packing just the right gear, and not overpacking with equipment that was not necessary. I jokingly looked around, wondering where the pile of discarded gear was that Mac left here in 1944. He felt that he was too overweighed and left a good belt axe, a pair of pants, extra shoes, a jar of salmon eggs, lead weights, two pounds of cheese, a small sack of flour, and a bag of salt. This shedding of gear left his pack ten pounds lighter. By today's standards, it would be unthinkable to ditch gear and litter along the trail in a national park, or anywhere in the woods for that matter.

Three grouse kept me entertained for a few minutes on the summit. They ran about, up and over rocks, around clumps of vegetation, getting closer and closer to me, seemingly comfortable and explorative. Mac had a similar experience with a brace of grouse standing in this very spot.

The air was cool and heavy with moisture. I was anxious to get down into the next valley for the night, but I gave up on my goal of getting to Rush Creek to camp as the sun was setting. I don't like trying to make camp in the dark. I found a good campsite in a shallow valley just below the pass that was well off the trail and tucked under a small clump of stunted trees just as darkness arrived.

Up before the sun and excited to get moving, I boiled water for my ritualistic cup of mocha. Growing up, my family always drank mocha in the mornings while backpacking. It is a simple mix of powdered hot chocolate and instant coffee. It was the only time as kids that we were allowed to drink coffee, so we thought it was a treat.

I gathered my stuff and stepped out to find the trail. I hadn't realized that the trail doubled back and I'd spent the night within five feet of it. And here, I thought, I was invisible and in solitude!

* * *

The creek draining the Marie Lakes was inviting. For about forty-five minutes, I fished upstream from where it crosses the trail. Using a Gray Hackle mosquito fly, I landed many small brookies up to seven inches. I did not make the hike to the lakes, but have since been told by several hikers along the trail that the fishing is good there.

In the first hour that I spent on the trail, I passed twenty-one people—*way* too many people for my comfort level. My entire backpacking life has been in areas and along trails that were quiet and out of the way. I remember as a kid it was very infrequent to pass another hiker. When it did happen, there was usually a mutual desire to spend a few minutes to sit and talk with one another, a kind of "Whoa, here is an opportunity to ask someone how the fishing was or what's up ahead on the trail," moment.

I made it to Island Pass by 10:30 with little effort; it really isn't much of a "pass," but more of a ridge that the trail traverses. I checked the map and took a compass heading for a cross-country route to the inlet creek of Thousand Island Lake. I had a notion that there would be big fish there. Mac used a Rio Grande King fly to successfully land thirteen large fish in the fifteen-inch class. The fish were some sort of hybrid with rainbow-like coloration and lateral bands, but with spots like the Loch Leven and cutthroat.

Approaching the lake, I found a prominent rock on which

to doff my pack, eat some lunch, and survey the lake. I fished the water's edge to the inlet on the west end of the lake at the foot of beautifully jagged Mount Banner. I had no strikes and never saw a fish larger than two inches. What happened to the "lunkers" that Mac talked about? He mentioned big fish that repeatedly bowed his rod sharply after a heavy underwater take. Usually, his big fish would take his line with short and savage rushes, bore to the bottom, and only rise when sheer exhaustion made it impossible to move a fin. I thought to myself that they might not be here anymore. Disappointed to find no big fish in the lake, I changed flies in rapid succession, from a grasshopper to an elk hair caddis, then to a yellow-bodied Stimulator, in hopes of catching *something*. No luck.

Banner Peak above Thousand Island Lake

On my way back to my pack, I stopped at a rock on a point that gave me a perfect casting platform. The water was shallow for the first thirty feet, then gave way to a deep trough about twenty feet wide. The water was clear, the trough a deep blue color. Try something different, I thought to myself. So I dug around in the bottom of my fly box and found a gold bead-headed, rust-colored, flashy leech. It was the only one like it in my fly box. My experience with wet fly fishing has been limited, as I enjoy fishing with dry flies. With dry flies, I can see where my fly is and watch the fish rise and take the offering.

The first cast landed the fly in the middle of the blue trough. The fly sank as I gave the line a little slack. Suddenly there was a sharp yank, and the loose line went taught. The fly line was coiled at my feet with about ten feet of slack when the fly hit the water. As the massive fish ran with my fly, the line zipped through my fingers too fast for me to react. The drag on my reel was set too tight, and when the slack line hit the reel, I could hear the snap of my tippet. Four-pound tippet was clearly no match for that fish.

Angry at myself but excited about the size of the fish that took my fly, I knew then and there that "lunkers" were in fact living in this lake. I dug through my fly box for another rust-colored leech, but finding nothing similar, I tied on a black Woolly Bugger and set off for another shot at that big guy. He was nowhere to be found, but I did hook into a fat, silvery twelve-inch rainbow that jumped four times as I brought him ashore. I have never seen a Sierra trout jump like that before. Exciting!

It was getting late in the afternoon and I had set my goal of camping at Garnet Lake for the night. I knew I wanted to fish the outlet of Thousand Island Lake again.

The last time I was here was during the summer of 1978 (thirty-four years ago) when Leon Borowski, my Monta Vista High School biology teacher, took a group of us students to study the geology, flora, and fauna of the Sierra, rock climb, and summit Mt. Ritter. It was a great trip that I took with my friends Steve Osborne and Richard Craig. During the trip, a kid in the class got sick, so I ran back to the ranger station to get help. Being one of the more experienced hikers and able to make the run back to the ranger station, I easily made the run to bring back help. Later on I sprained my ankle and could not climb Mt. Ritter. Disappointed, I had to stay back at camp to recover.

Thousand Island twelve-inch rainbow

During that trip, I hiked down the outlet of Thousand Island Lake where the creek dove into a chasm on its way to the Middle Fork of the San Joaquin River. At one point, I held my fly rod in my teeth as I climbed down into a gorge to gain access to a few nice pools. Fishing those pools was some of the best fishing I have ever experienced in my life, and I caught several big fish. They were trapped in the gorge and couldn't get out. It was very memorable for me and I wanted to repeat it.

With the memories of the big fish I had caught in the gorge swimming through my mind, I walked down canyon about a mile, but could not find any type of gorge. The outlet creek just cascaded down the side of the granite valley below with no gorge in sight. Could it be the wrong lake? My memory was that it was the Thousand Island Lake outlet. Perplexed and defeated, I vowed to keep my memory the same: it was the outlet from Thousand Island Lake where I caught those fish thirty-four years ago. I set off to Garnet Lake to camp instead.

I only made it as far as Ruby Lake when it started to rain. Not wanting to repeat the event of hiking in the rain like I had two days ago, I pitched the tarp on the edge of the peaceful, aptly named gem of a lake. Ruby Lake is a deep green-blue color, and only the rain dimples broke its surface. It was so quiet and still that evening, it almost wiped away my frustration with the crowds I experienced earlier that day.

Ruby Lake

It was this lake that Mac stumbled upon while trying to find the trail through a series of snow banks in 1944. At that time, the lake was unnamed. He found small, lazy trout swimming about, but apparently it hadn't been worth investigating since he didn't even wet a fly here.

The sun was shining on the top half of the cliffs along the west side of Ruby Lake when I stepped out onto the trail the next morning. Walking along the lake's edge revealed only a few small rising fish as they cruised along the bank. Otherwise, the water was as smooth as glass, the air perfectly still.

Garnet Lake was a short and easy hike of only a few miles. It was flat and calm in the still morning air as I walked along the trail overlooking the elegant body of water with a near-perfect reflection of the minarets. I fished the outlet of the lake until the cataracts became too difficult to traverse. Brookies and rainbows up to nine inches were plentiful and took my green-bodied Stimulator without hesitation. I hooked into one feisty nine-inch brookie in a small pool almost a half-mile down the outlet stream. He darted about from one side of the pool to the other, and then attempted to jump the falls just to get away.

Shadow Creek was the next stop that I had marked on my map as a possible good fishing experience. Arriving at 10:30, I took the opportunity to soak my feet and snack on some jerky and dried fruit. Also resting at the creek were two older gentlemen, brothers named Jim and Tony. Tony lives in San Diego and has a condo in Mammoth Lakes, and Jim now lives in Pennsylvania. They were hiking out to Agnew Meadows to catch the shuttle to Tony's condo near the center of town. We chatted for a while and they suggested that I hike with them out to the shuttle that would take me to Reds Meadow Resort. I was initially thinking of sticking to the John Muir Trail and fishing Minaret Creek at Johnston Meadow. They seemed to think that the fishing there was not worth the trek and offered for me to join them for dinner at a Thai restaurant in town. I declined their generous offer because I was looking forward to experiencing Reds Meadow Resort's food and atmosphere.

Sitting on the bank of Shadow Creek with my feet dangling in the cold water, I made the decision to stash my pack, don my Teva sandals, and head for Ediza Lake to explore the fishing. From there I would hike to Agnew Meadows to catch the last shuttle to Reds Meadow at 7:00 p.m. for dinner. I did the two miles to Ediza Lake in forty minutes. It was an easy hike, and I stopped at a few nice pools to fish in Shadow Creek. The pools were full of small brookies and rainbows to eight inches.

Ediza Lake

Ediza Lake is a beautiful slice of water sitting at the base of the Minarets. I wanted to visit this lake, seeing as it was the site of the base camp for the search crew that was looking for missing hiker Walter A. Starr, Jr. in 1933. Some of the best mountain climbers of the time were assembled, including Norman Clyde, Jules Eichorn, Glen Dawson, Richard Jones, and Oliver Kehrlein. Starr's camp was found near here and his climbing gear was missing, so the focus of the search took place in the Minarets.

Starr was a Stanford graduate and respected lawyer from San Francisco. He ventured out to explore the Sierra and was preparing a guidebook, but never returned. The official search was suspended after five or six days; finding a body in the Minarets was like finding a needle in a haystack.

Norman Clyde (arguably the best mountaineer and climber in the Sierra at the time) was a good friend and frequent climbing partner of Starr's. He could not give up the search. He thought that his friend was still on the mountain somewhere, which continued to eat at him. Without supplies, funding, or assistance, Norman Clyde continued to survey the Minarets. He eventually found Walter's body on a ledge where it lay after a significant fall. His body was eventually interned on that ledge and still remains there today. William Alsup's *Missing in the Minarets* is an exquisite narrative of the events and circumstances surrounding Starr's disappearance and the subsequent search for his body.

The wind began to blow and I sat on a rock at the edge of the lake, taking in every bit of the view that I could. Wanting to make the shuttle to Reds Meadow, I figured I should at least wet a fly before leaving such an amazing place. I had an elk hair caddis on the end of my leader and I cast toward a submerged rock. The fly landed on the water, and almost immediately I spotted a dark figure swimming up from the depths toward it. He zigzagged several times before taking my fly. Giving him plenty of line and time, I played him until he was too tired (he was a fat fourteen-inch rainbow). Since I was planning on dinner at Reds Meadow Resort, I released him after taking a picture.

Soon after, I was back on the trail to pick up my pack. I made good time down to the junction of the John Muir Trail and

Shadow Creek and passed by Shadow Lake without fishing. I imagine it to be a popular destination since it is an easy day hike from Agnew Meadows. Catching up with Jim and Tony at the River Trail Junction, I hiked with them the rest of the way to Agnew Meadows. We had some great conversations, and I very much enjoyed getting to know these two gentlemen. We somehow got on the subject of water treatment as I struggled to keep up with them (I was pushing twelve miles at this time and still had a few more to go). They use a filter and a SteriPEN (a portable battery powered devise that uses ultraviolet light to sterilize the water). Both were very concerned about contracting giardia from untreated water, and they were genuinely uneasy for me since I was not treating my water at all, something I feel is unnecessary (more on this subject later).

I made it to Reds Meadow Resort with plenty of time to make reservations for the daily dinner special. The resort consists of a restaurant, general store, cabins for rent, and a campground. Hot showers and laundry services are also available to the hikers and guests. The campground at the resort was a quarter-mile walk from the restaurant and general store. I was directed to the section that is set aside for hikers by the campground host. She drove around in a golf cart and seemed to keep a keen eye on all of the comings and goings within the backpackers' section of the campground. Her gruff exterior and demeanor gave me the impression that she did not particularly like the backpackers. I picked out an empty site with a fireplace and gathered up enough firewood for the night. About a half dozen other backpackers had descended upon the campground and settled in, busily organizing their packs and gear with their new food purchased at the general store. Reds Meadow Resort is also a popular food drop location where many backpackers will send a food cache ahead of time for their next hiking section. I met Taka, a twenty-five-year-old Japanese student and a solo John Muir Trail through-hiker, and offered to camp with me and split the cost of the site for the night. As it turned out, he was a complete novice backpacker and started his trek at Yosemite's Half Dome with brand new gear.

There is an interesting phenomenon that surrounds long distance backpackers. A kind of an instant kinship develops quickly and seems to be deep with meaning. Names and stories are shared on the trail, and here, over a meal, a sense of camaraderie and closeness is kindled.

Many through-hikers have a "trail name." Some names are earned, others self-imposed, and for some the name is thrust upon them. For most, the new name is a sort of reflection of their camp or trail habits, hometown, hiking style, or food choices, or reflects an event that the hiker experienced. Maybe it is a way to escape home life, or perhaps a desire to seek a new identity while the hiker reinvents his or her inner self. Either way, it often makes for some interesting talk alongside the trail.

I had the pleasure of enjoying the daily special of beef stew with several other hikers. I shared a table with Taka, who now resides in Southern California, Kevin from Sun River, Oregon, Alan from New Jersey, and Tom and his adult kids from La Honda, California. We had a wonderful meal while swapping stories and getting to know each other, and the cold beer tasted all too good.

CHAPTER 2

Reds Meadow to Mono Creek

Ten Most Beautiful Places in the Sierras
(not in order)

1. *Evolution Valley*
2. *Le Conte Canyon*
3. *Lyell Fork of the Tuolumne River Valley*
4. *Humphreys Basin—desolate but impressive*
5. *The Minarets near Lake Ediza*
6. *Rae Lakes, if you get rid of 95% of the people*
7. *Lake of the Lone Indian and the surrounding area*
8. *Upper Evolution Valley*
9. *Tyndall Creek drainage area*
10. *Kern River Valley*

As I walked out of Reds Meadow Resort and past the horse corral and pack station, I found myself standing on the edge of the 1992 Rainbow Fire. The scars from the fire stretched for miles in all directions. The telltale signs of charred, still-standing trees and new growth vegetation were startling. Reds Resort had been spared, however.

The fire started on August 20, 1992, under extreme weather conditions. Lightning ignited the drought-stricken vegetation and quickly spread, as it was being fanned by sixty-mile per hour winds. In the end, almost 9,000 acres of the national forest and Devil's Postpile National Monument were burned.

Climbing out of the valley, it was also easy to see the hundreds of thousands of trees that blew down in a major windstorm the previous November. The greater Devil's Postpile area was hit with a storm that produced winds up to 150 miles per hour. The trail crews had been very busy cutting the trees away from the trails and roads in the area. Between the fire and the windstorm, the area had been hit hard, and was fighting even harder to bounce back.

Rainbow Fire and windstorm damage south of Reds Meadow

I stopped at Crater Creek to fish. It was a trickle of a creek, choked with brush and vegetation and full of small fish. I had to work hard to get to a few of the more productive pools. I caught three fish, one measuring eight inches and two considerably smaller. All three had a red stripe along the lateral line, with red gill plates and a small orange patch on the belly. Other than white-tipped anal fins, they had no other distinguishing marks.

The largest of the three had swallowed my fly, and it was lodged deep enough in his throat that I couldn't extricate the hook without harming him. I kept the fish and gave it to Taka for his dinner. He happened to be passing me as I came back to my pack after fishing the small creek. He was very excited.

As I rounded the corner, on the trail just a few hundred yards away from Crater Creek, I was given the gift of the last view of the Minarets of the Ritter Range. What a beautiful sight! They are an impressive group of granite peaks.

On the way to Duck Creek, it started to rain *again*. Thunder made its presence known in the distance, but I never saw any lightning. While hiking this long stretch of trail with great views of the valley below and mountains above, I remembered how Dad would tell stories and try to convince us that he used to be Paul Bunyan in a past life. He did this to keep our minds off the long hike we were in the middle of. He would say things like, "See that dead tree standing there with no branches? I would pick those up and use them as toothpicks," or, "See that splotch of white on that cliff? That was where I spat my toothpaste and it stained the rocks white." Another favorite was how much of the ground features and valleys were "carved" by his blue ox, Babe, when they would play. I don't think we were ever convinced, but his ploy worked. We always made it to our destination before we knew it.

Gliding into Duck Creek exhausted, and with very sore feet, I had only one goal on my mind: take my boots off and rest. How was it that Mac came this entire way wearing hobnail boots during his first trip in 1944? Hobnails are short, thickheaded nails that are inserted into the sole of a boot to allow the wearer better traction on soft ground. Often they are worn by lumbermen to prevent them from slipping off logs. He often complained that the hobnails were as slippery as ice when walking on the sierra granite.

Campsites at Duck Creek were minimal and rudimentary at best. Level ground was at a premium, and I had to search a bit to find a site suitable to pitch the tarp. It was raining off and on, and I didn't want to get caught in the middle of the night without shelter. I ate a quick freeze-dried dinner and fell fast asleep within minutes.

I woke that morning after the best night's sleep so far on the trip. Up until now, I had been plagued with leg cramps at night and struggled to get used to sleeping on my pad. It made for restless sleeping, until that night. By eight o'clock, I was off to fish the famous Duck Lake with images of seventeen-inch rainbow and golden trout dancing in my head. I made quick time hiking up to the lake without my pack.

With the sun still low on the horizon and just above the surrounding peaks, a slight mist rose from the water. The air was dead calm and the water crystal clear. I chose to skirt around and fish the south side of the lake because it looked deeper and appeared to be an easier traverse. After an hour of casting, scrambling, and switching flies, my line continued to come up empty. Skunked! Not even a single strike. Heck, I never saw a fish larger than four inches.

At one point in his career, Mac worked at the Emporium in San Francisco in the old Cabin Sports Shop. A customer once approached the fishing tackle counter and requested well-tied flies for the giants of Duck Lake. The customer proceeded to report to Mac that Duck Lake was known to harbor big fish. Mac was determined, then and there, to one day visit Duck Lake and search for those legendary golden trout. Mac did visit the lake in 1944 and used a variety of fishing techniques to coax the big fish. He bent a snelled Royal Coachman on the dropper of a yellow-bodied Gray Hackle fly. He ended up with two fish at once, both rainbows. Eventually, he landed a fat seventeen-inch golden trout.

Discouraged, I headed back to my pack and was soon off to Purple Lake. Just before reaching Purple Lake, I passed a hiker on the trail who said the water was "boiling" in the morning with rising fish. That got me excited, and I was ready to catch some fish after the Duck Lake disappointment. When I arrived at the lake, there was a hunting party fishing along the south side. They had a dog with them that was running about, barking, and jumping into the water. Since the lake is quite small, the annoying sounds carried all too well throughout the cliffs surrounding the lake, and it began to wear on my nerves. Halfway around the north side of the lake, where the vegetation and big rocks made travel more difficult, I gave up.

One cast into Purple Lake

When I got back to the outlet creek where the trail crosses, Taka and Alan were there resting and watching me fish. Since leaving Tuolumne Meadows, I had been "leap-frogging" with them and several other hikers. Our pace must have been similar, and we would often find ourselves hiking together for a while. It was a good feeling to see a familiar face every once in a while.

Taka wanted me to catch him another fish for his dinner, so I walked out onto the logs piled up against the outlet. A few fish were rising to bugs on the surface and slowly swimming about. Taka took a video as I made a few false casts to get my fly out to where the fish were feeding. The moment the fly landed on the water, a nine-inch golden leaped at my fly. Taka was amazed that it took only one cast to land that fish. After a few pictures, I cleaned it and gave it to him. Again, he was going to have fish for dinner and could not have been more exited.

I eventually said goodbye to Taka and Alan and set off for Virginia Lake. Just as I rounded the bend in the trail before the lake, Alan caught up with me. We stopped to eat some lunch before I set out to fish its southeast corner. I fished from three different rocks, using a yellow-bodied Simulator with no luck. The lake bottom dropped off quickly, so I switched to a rust-colored leech pattern that had some flashy tinsel to act as a tail. On the first retrieve, a large shadow darted toward my fly like a torpedo. It was a drive-by. I had two more and a strong strike before landing a gorgeous thirteen-inch golden trout. I was standing on a tall rock at the edge of the lake and mentally struggled with how best to land the fighter. Glancing behind me, I noticed a fishing net between the rocks, obviously lost by a fisherman years ago. Thankfully, I was able to grab it and land the fish. Perfect timing. I left the net sitting on top of a rock for the next fisherman.

I had several more drive-bys and a few more strikes before the rain, hail, and thunder drove me away. Alan had stayed to watch me fish and enjoyed the show, but we both wanted to get to Tully Hole to camp and have a fire for the evening. I hated to leave such a productive lake and wanted to fish all the way around it, but there were more lakes to explore. Besides, the rain told me that it was time to leave. Alan and I scrambled to get our raingear on, then made the trek out of the lake basin and onward to Tully Hole.

The rain and hail kept pounding harder and harder. Soon, the trail became a river. Then there were rivers where there shouldn't have been. Alan and I stumbled into a wooded area next to Fish Creek, and not far behind us came Pete, a China Lake fireman, and Ray and Yanka, two nurses from Arizona. We all stood under my tarp for a couple of hours until the rain finally subsided. It is amazing how well you get to know your new friends when sheltered from a storm in the backcountry. We told stories, explored each other's pasts, and shared some warm drinks while watching the water level rise in Fish Creek. By dinnertime, the creek was a rushing, muddy torrent that must have risen five feet above normal flow.

Fourteen-inch golden from Virginia Lake

Without dry wood to make a fire, we decided to break out our stoves and eat our own dinners together since the rain had slowed to a slight drizzle. I cooked the three trout from Purple Lake and Virginia Lake over the stove to share with the group. My clothes were sodden, and I hung them on a tree branch that was in the driest spot. Not wanting to get my dry clothes wet, too, I turned in early. The rest of the group soon followed.

It was a cool and damp morning the next day. Everything was still wet, and wringing out my clothes, sleeping bag, and gear took a while. My pack must have gained an extra five pounds from all the wet gear.

Fish Creek was still rushing, although the water level had dropped markedly overnight. That morning the clarity of the creek had improved a great deal, but still was not fishable.

Just after the bridge above Cascade Valley, I stopped and talked briefly to a camper that was packing up. He said he had caught brookies and brightly colored rainbows the previous day before the rainstorm hit.

Halfway up to Squaw Lake, I stopped to fish the creek draining the lake where the trail crosses the creek. It took just a few minutes to land three or four small brookies using a green-bodied Stimulator.

Squaw Lake offered a half-dozen brookies to nine inches in about fifteen minutes. What a pleasant fishing spot. Though the fish were small, there were enough to keep any fly angler happy for a while. It made for a good break from the climb up the hill, too.

Where the trail to Lake of the Lone Indian and Goodale Pass takes off from the John Muir Trail, I doffed my pack and laid all my wet clothes and gear on the rocks to dry. The sun was shining and the air was warm. It was an odd thing to me to lay out all of my things in the open and walk away for several hours. I was not concerned that someone would take my stuff, but when everything is spread out on a rock in the sun to dry, who knows what could happen? It was sunny, my gear needed to dry, and, hell, I wanted to fish.

With my lunch in hand, I ventured off to Papoose Lake and Lake of the Lone Indian. Papoose Lake was full of brookies to ten inches. This small and shallow lake swarmed with fish. Mac had only found tadpoles and caddis larvae, and he felt that fish could not survive here because they would freeze during the winter months. A white and black Stimulator worked well for me to entice these small and spirited fish. Switching to a green leech with a split shot also proved to be productive. The leech really excited the bigger fish.

Papoose Lake

While sitting on the edge of Papoose Lake in the sun-soaked grass and eating my lunch, I began to wonder about the current state of this small lakelet. Why did Mac only find pollywogs and caddis larvae? Why are there only brook trout here now? I suppose that, in 1944, this small body of water was untouched by the fish planting programs of the Department of Fish and Game and the local packers.

Steve Beck, author of the book *Trout Fishing the John Muir Trail*, mentions that the "Indian Lakes" had been stocked with brook and rainbow trout, starting in 1934. Historically, these alpine lakes were fishless and mostly inhabited by several species of frogs. Perhaps Papoose Lake was not stocked until after Mac visited in 1944. I found myself deep in thought and speculation, and wanted only to lie back on the grassy bank and take a nap in the sun.

Pushing back the desires of a lazy afternoon, I scurried over to the rim overlooking Lake of the Lone Indian. A faint trail made its way down alongside the feeding creek to the lake's edge. A white Muddler proved to get the fish the most electrified. I had dozens of hard strikes from large twelve- to fourteen-inch fish that shot up from the depths to attack my fly. They would hit the fly, then dart back down as quickly as they had arrived. This was some of the most exciting fishing for me so far.

When Mac arrived here at this beautiful and solitary piece of heaven, he found tadpoles, caddis larvae, and big fish that mostly ignored his offerings. Mac wrote:

> *Useless though it appeared to try for those satiated fish, I took my rod along as I started a circuit of the lake after breakfast. Using long, fine tippeted leaders, I floated dry flies, sank wet ones, and even put on a bass bug in an effort to tempt those trout. I appealed to their curiosity and tried to arouse their combative instincts. All to no avail. Occasionally one would rise languidly, inspect my*

offering with indolent disdain, and then fin away heavily.

At least I got a strike or two out of them just to keep it interesting for me. I could have stayed and could spend an entire week just figuring out these artful dodgers, if I only had the time.

The clouds were starting to build and I wanted to get back to my gear on the rocks and over Silver Pass before it decided to rain again. Leaving Chief and Warrior Lakes without fishing was hard to do. Vowing to come back again some day, I turned and headed toward the pass after gathering all my now-dry gear.

Lake of the Lone Indian

At the top of Silver Pass, I formally met the camper that I had talked to near the bridge in Cascade Valley earlier in the morning. His name was Dan and he was backpacking with his eighty-year-old mother, Joanne. What an inspiration she was! We stayed on top of the pass for about forty-five minutes talking and sharing stories. They were backpacking the John Muir Trail in sections; this was their fourth section. They had already climbed Half Dome and Mt. Whitney. Now they just needed to fill in the middle parts. Dan is a fisheries biologist with the United States Forest Service in Bend, Oregon, and Joanne lives in Morgan Hill. Dan was very interested to hear about my trip, what I found so far, and a little about Mac's book. I gave him the information on the book and he assured me that he would somehow find a copy.

Dan and his eighty-year-old mother, Joanne

Dan and I planned to fish Silver Pass Lake when we got there. The wind kicked up as we both tackled the south and east shore of the lake. Mac was chased off this lake (unnamed back then) by an icy and windy storm and thus never fished here. Both Dan and I came up empty handed with only one strike. Dan jokingly said the fishing was lousy because it was 2:45 in the afternoon and it was windy.

The long hike down to Mono Creek took its toll on me. My feet, especially the balls of my feet, were raw, and I was forced to finish the last four and a half miles in my sandals. The long periods of downhill just did not agree with me, and I frequently stopped to let my feet soak in whatever water I crossed.

Mono Creek is a familiar and very enjoyable location for me. The last two summers, Heidi, the kids, and I have explored this area and enjoyed the splendid fishing these waters provide. Last year we caught four trout species from this creek and its tributaries within this lower section: brown, brook, rainbow, and golden trout. A United States Forest Service work crew had taken over the area we usually camp, so I was forced to find another spot. It was nearing dusk when I made camp, built a fire, and settled down for a dinner of chili with blueberry muffins for desert. It was nice to be cooking by a fire and enjoying the company of the flames. I slept not too far from the creek that night, so the sounds of the rushing water worked well as a tranquilizer to help put me to sleep.

CHAPTER 3

Mono Creek to Florence Lake

I woke this morning to the sun shining on the Vermillion Cliffs. Simply spectacular! I fished Mono Creek for about fifteen minutes and landed two brown trout. One was eight inches and the other was a fat and muscular twelve inches. The big guy took a bead-headed nymph dropped from a grasshopper.

The water on this stretch of creek is typically fast and gin-clear, with perfect flow over boulders and great pocket water. It's always a challenge to get your fly where you need it. This makes for a great fishing experience that I keep coming back to year after year. It was nice to be back on familiar water. There are several perfect pools that I have fished the last few years, and I've always been successful with large fish.

It was around noon and I was sitting on top of Bear Ridge, leaning up against a big lodgepole pine. The year before, in this very same spot, I was presented with the best margarita I have ever had. It was my fiftieth birthday. It had been a heavy winter the previous season, and the snow on the ridge was still thick. Heidi and I found a great patch of snow and she brought out powdered lemonade, tequila, and a fresh lime. Mixed with snow and served in my Sierra cup, it was a memory that I will never forget.

Unfortunately, there were so many hikers on this section of trail. You can hear them coming for miles, the *tick tick tick* sound they make as their metal-tipped trekking poles hit the rocks along the trail. I have noticed that most hikers and backpackers are now using these trekking poles. When asked, they usually will tell me that it improves their stability, steadies their weight, and adds additional propulsion to their stride. There are maybe forty hikers a day along this section, and I think just about half of them passed me in a half hour as I sat there writing.

* * *

As I trudged up to the top of Bear Ridge from the Mono Creek drainage, I particularly enjoyed following the change of tree species. It seemed to keep my mind off the 2,000-foot climb in elevation. The Mono Creek area is full of huge Jeffrey pine, red fir, and quaking aspen. As the trail climbs up the ridge, the forest's combination of trees changes to mostly hemlock and white bark pine, then to white fir, and finally to almost pure stands of lodgepole pine on the ridge crest.

I found a perfect campsite alongside the Hilgard Branch of Bear Creek, about two miles up the trail toward Lake Italy. Arriving at 3:30 in the afternoon, I immediately went to work starting a fire, boiling water, setting up a washbasin, and doing my laundry. I learned from my parents how to make a great washbasin for doing dishes, washing clothes, or bathing. A three foot square piece of plastic sheeting is placed over a circle of rocks. The water is poured in and, *voila*, you have an instant washbasin.

The sun was shining and it was peaceful and warm, so I took this opportunity to take a bath. With all the domestic chores completed, I set off to fish upstream from camp. It swarmed with small golden trout. All were bright and beautiful and seemed to attack every dry fly pattern I tossed their way.

My camp was perched on top of a smooth slab of granite that gradually sloped down to the water's edge. The remnants of an old fire pit were visible on top of the slab, so I re-assembled the fire ring, made a big fire, moved a few of the bigger and flatter rocks around to make a usable kitchen, and made a perfect "Heidi Chair" next to the fire. A "Heidi Chair" is a backcountry piece of furniture built for the situation, using whatever materials are at hand to be comfortable at camp. On our first backpack trip into the Trinity Alps, Heidi made me a couch. She used a log as the backrest, dug out a seat in the dirt, and lined it with our sleeping pads and sleeping bags. It was right next to the fire, and I was the most comfortable I had ever been in camp while backpacking.

Camp at Hilgard Branch

* * *

Mac talks a lot about his gear and the equipment he used during his excursions. As one of the first authors to write a bestselling fishing book, he took the opportunity to expose his readers to backpacking in the Sierra Nevada. Comparing his gear, equipment, and fishing tackle reveals a vast array of advancements in today's equipment and reveals how truly tough he was.

Mac used a "packboard" during his trips. I am only guessing that it was a wooden structure onto which his gear was lashed or stowed in an attached sack. I remember seeing, when I was a kid, a similar packboard that my dad had. He made it when he was in Boy Scouts and used it on several backpacking trips as a young boy. I imagine that the two were very similar. I use a Jansport external frame pack that I bought when my son Justin and I went on his first backpack trip when he was five years old, making this pack about twenty years old. It is well worn, with a patch on a pocket where a mouse or rat chewed its way in to get food scraps, but it is comfortably purposeful.

Many John Muir Trail backpackers are ultra-light fanatics and use a variety of small, lightweight packs and simple gear constructed of newer, more lightweight materials—down sleeping bags, for instance. On Mac's first trip, he took a wool sleeping bag that was most likely very heavy, and by his own admission was very cold during some of the coldest nights he experienced. During his second and third backpack trips, he used a new down sleeping bag. He had made several references to its much-improved warmth. I use a down sleeping bag made by Marmot that I have had for about twelve years. I have noticed that the down tends to move around in the sleeves, and when unzipped and draped over me like a quilt (my preferred sleeping method), the down moves off the top of me and settles to the sides. This makes for a cold night's sleep during the coldest weather. I usually resort to zipping up the bag mummy style—something I find too confining for my likes, but is much warmer.

Mac would cut boughs from trees, gather pine needles, and lie directly on the ground. He never used any sort of sleeping pad or ground cloth, another testament to the toughness of this man. I used a new sleeping pad system for this trip and found that it worked great. I use two pads. The top pad is a three-quarter-length Thermarest air and foam pad, and beneath it is a quarter-inch closed foam pad. Over both of them is a slipcover sheet that I sewed to fit. I would lie directly on that with the bag draped over me. This system works very well and usually keeps me comfortable and warm.

Mac wore boots with hobnail soles on his first trip in 1944. It made for interesting conversation when other trail users followed his footprints. During his subsequent trips, he wore boots with a "composition sole made of rubber and cord, called 'Glo-cord soles.'" I wear a new pair of Asolo boots (made in Italy). I worked them in for several months prior to the trip, and I am still convinced that heavy leather upper boots are the best footwear for the High Sierra backpacker. So many ultra-light backpackers are now wearing a variation of a running shoe, which I feel does not provide adequate protection or support for the foot.

In the mid-1940s, cooking was always done over a fire. There were no fire restrictions at that time. Mac carried and used a "stewpan" in which he cooked all his meals. I use a fire (my preferred choice) unless regulations dictate otherwise. So far, most of the time I have not been allowed to make a fire and have been forced to cook over my gas Whisperlight stove made by MSR. These fire restrictions tend to leave me in a state of awkwardness. Since I grew up backpacking and always cooking with fire, it has become almost ritualistic and is always the most comfortable for me. I feel the regulations are not so much of a wildfire threat as they are a way to slowly modify the behaviors of the backcountry visitors to not use fire. Rangers and maintenance personnel are tired of cleaning foil and trash from fire pits and take every opportunity to tear them down and restrict the use of campfires.

Both Mac and I use a tarp for shelter. I have never backpacked with a tent. That was how we did it when I was a kid and it has stuck with me. It is also partly a weight reduction issue, as well as the tranquility of seeing and sleeping with the stars overhead. My friend Greg Meyer (a marine biology professor and outdoor educator) turned me on to a new product for a ground cloth: a piece of Tyvek. Tyvek is a very strong, lightweight vapor barrier used in the construction industry as part of the exterior wall system. It works great.

A trusty wool shirt was the only mention of the clothes that Mac brought on his trips. Several pictures show him wearing what appeared to be denim jeans, cuffed high around his boot tops. For all my trips growing up, a wool shirt was standard. We all had to have one, and the Pendleton brand was our favorite. Mom was also known to sew us our own shirts. Sometimes she would remove the tag from an old Pendleton shirt and sew it into one of the ones she made just to make us feel good, like we were wearing the real thing. Like we didn't know! While getting ready for one of my Boy Scout backpack trips, my mom gave me a pair of jeans that she wanted me to take. They had been modified, Barbara style, with suede leather patches on the knees and butt. She insisted that I always seemed to come back with holes in my jeans in those areas. I objected, but my objections did not get very far with Mom, so the jeans went for a ride in my backpack, never to be worn on the entire trip. Instead, I wore my spare pair during the trip. Stubborn, aren't I? Now, I hike in a Hawaiian shirt. It is light, thin, and dries quickly. I most certainly was the only hiker wearing one, and I am sure that I was the envy of all other hikers.

I can only imagine the weight and bulk of the camera equipment that Mac carried on his trips. He carried a variety of accessories, including lenses, filters, a tripod, and rolls of extra film. I use a small Fuji digital camera from Costco and a small three-inch tripod.

It seems that most people along the trail ask how the fishing is when they see that I am carrying a fishing rod. I have met very few fly anglers along the way. Those that I have met are very interested in my success and will freely provide me with the stories of their triumphs. On one day, I walked with a guy named Joe (from North Carolina) for a mile or so. We talked fishing, flies, rods, and reels, only to find out that he was a complete novice fly angler and had never fished (let alone visited) California. Before we parted ways, he got out his fly box and I pointed out which flies would work best in this area. I gave him one of my strike indicators to use with his wet flies. He was very excited, and I wished him luck as we went our separate ways.

That evening I cooked a generous meal of trout with bacon bits, and then followed that with a cup of chili and cheddar garlic mashed potatoes. I was stuffed. My camp was about two miles away from the John Muir Trail and made for a quiet and peaceful evening with no one around—just how I prefer my backcountry trips.

* * *

I made it to Lake Italy (1,500 feet in three and a half miles) by eleven o'clock in the morning. Because the maintenance and use of the trail was minimal at best, I kept losing and then finding the trail again. Even when I would give up and set a cross-country route, I would somehow stumble back onto the trail.

As I crested the rocky moraine holding the lake's water back, a huge immature bald eagle soared not more than twenty feet over my head. I stood there in awe as he glided with the wind currents from one side of the canyon to the other. What a majestic animal. I paused and wondered what the view would be like from his vantage point.

As I crossed the outlet creek of Lake Italy, I could see small fish darting about, spooked by my presence. Mac was right: this was a very barren, treeless, and windy place. There wasn't a tree or bush in sight.

Lake Italy at 11,202 feet

With my rod rigged with a black furry fly with white rubber "legs," I approached the first opportunity to cast into a deep section. My thoughts still went to the big steelhead Mac found here seventy years ago. Numerous casts and retrieves brought only strikes from twelve-inchers. I worked my way around the south shore to keep the wind at my left shoulder. It is much easier to cast when the wind blows from that direction or directly at my back. If the wind were off my right shoulder, it would blow my fly back into my body.

When I switched to a white and red Muddler fly, the first cast brought a hard strike and I hooked a beautiful rainbow-looking trout. As I brought it in, the dorsal fin looked strange. It was erect, flared, and shaped like a parallelogram. After subsequent investigations during my trip, I realized that the shape was normal for trout in the Sierra. I guess I had been looking for some oddity in the fish, given Mac's experience with the "steelheads."

I continued around the south end of the lake while switching flies regularly. I focused on different leech patterns and colors. On the return trip, I used only dry flies and switched flies often in an attempt to find the right pattern, color, size, and shape.

In all, I landed eight fish, nothing over eleven inches or smaller than nine inches. They all were beautiful goldens, except for the first rainbow. All the fish were quite thin and spirited. Strangely, for every fish I hooked I must have had ten strikes. Lake Italy trout are lousy at catching their food—maybe that is why they're so skinny!

Lake Italy golden trout

Mac found big silvery fish "as bright as any fresh run half-pounder ever taken from the Klamath River." He originally thought they were steelhead, but there was no way that a rainbow trout could have traveled out to sea and back. Mac deduced that, "obviously someone must have planted steelhead fry in Lake Italy." He went on to conclude that the fish had "grown and remained silvery instead of reverting to a rainbow coloration. Accordingly, to me, steelhead must be a separate and distinct species, not just any rainbow that has gone to sea and returned."

Why did Mac find steelhead seventy years ago, whereas I only found one rainbow and mostly golden trout? What impact has the Department of Fish and Game had on this lake or others in this part of the Sierra? Did they plant golden trout here? Have all of Mac's steelheads died off?

I remember as a kid being at lakes when the Department of Fish and Game planes would fly by and drop thousands of fish fingerlings into the lake to plant it. That was exciting. Local ranchers and fishermen have also been known to transplant fish from one body of water to another. There are so many possibilities, and we may never know the true impacts of all those efforts.

When Mac visited this barren alpine lake in 1945, he continued on to attempt to traverse the pass to look down into Granite Park on the other side. For him, an enormous snow bank, unscalable cliffs, and the lack of a trail proved too much, and he turned around. There is just no way that I could physically do that in one day. Instead, I diverted over to Teddy Bear and Brown Bear Lakes.

The outlet creek from Teddy Bear Lake had a few small fish swimming in one pool. Naturally, my thoughts were encouraging about the possibility of big fish. These are small lakes that require a cross-country trek to visit. Maybe little or no angling pressure has made for a population of big fish.

As I walked up to the small lakelet (Teddy Bear Lake), it was obvious that it was shallow, and the bottom rocks were very mossy. The color of the moss was close to a lime-green hue. Strange! I cast a few times just to humor myself and found the lake devoid of any life. Brown Bear Lake was the same: fishless. Not even a bug or larvae seemed to inhabit the body of water. I would think that of the two lakes, Brown Bear could harbor a trout population—it was deep, clear, and had only a small amount of moss. What's more, the outlet creek contained a number of fish. Another mystery.

I got back to camp at 4:30 and decided to pack up and head to Rosemarie Meadow. That way I could get an earlier start in the morning to visit Rose Lake, which lies just a mile off the John Muir Trail. As I approached Rosemarie Meadow, Taka and another young hiker were attempting to ford a small creek. They had hiked out to Vermillion Valley Resort at Lake Edison several days earlier, needing to restock their food supply and replace some equipment. Normally, that trek is easier since most through-hikers will catch the ferry across the lake to get to the resort. But since it was a very dry year, the water level of the lake was too low to allow the ferry service to continue. They were then forced to hike around the lake, adding another ten miles to their trip.

Taka and his hiking partner were very tired and eager to get to Rosemarie Meadow to set up camp and get a good night's sleep. It was nearing dusk when we walked up to the first level spot next to the trail that would make a good campsite. They invited me to join them, but I declined due to my desire to get away from the trail and find a little peace and quiet. But really, the only spots to sleep were in a series of shallow depressions. I avoid those at all costs.

I camped just up the trail, next to the creek on a good flat spot beside a big boulder. There was plenty of firewood, a good view of the meadow, and the sounds of the creek to lull me to sleep. I settled in to make a fine campsite, complete with a big fire and a comfortable Heidi Chair from which to enjoy it. I settled down to write in my journal and enjoyed the evening fire. The stars were out, and I was very tired when I finally turned in for the night. When I turned out my headlamp, there was a flash.

At first I thought my eyes were playing tricks on me. After I turned out my headlamp, I laid there in the dark thinking it was just my eyes adjusting to the darkness and that it was no big deal.

Nope! It was lightning off in the distance, beyond the mountains to the southeast. I watched it flashing, and when no thunder sounded, I knew it was too far away to be of concern to me.

I thought back to a trip to Baja California, Mexico, with Heidi a few years ago. We were at a beachfront restaurant in Mulege. As we sat at a table on the beach eating dinner and drinking margaritas, the sun was setting as we watched the lightning show across the Sea of Cortez, possibly over mainland Mexico. We enjoyed the spectacular and very romantic spectacle for several hours until the storm hit us. We scrambled to help the owners and staff get the tables and chairs inside before they blew away. Then we battened down the hatches. The storm hit hard, with considerable wind gusts, rain, and thunder and lightning all around us. It was terrifying initially, but turned into a party afterwards.

Last night was the same. I lay there admiring it from a distance until it began to rain. I scrambled to get the tarp erected as the raindrops grew bigger. Then I was getting pelted by hail the size of M&Ms. Once the wind began to blow from the wrong direction, I knew that the Sierra Nevada was welcoming me as only she can do. I had pitched the tarp up against a big rock for better protection, but leaving two sides open didn't do much to keep the wetness out. The rain and wind continued all night.

The assault of the rain, lightning, thunder, hail, and wind kept me up throughout the night. Just to make things worse, my tarp failed. At first, I thought it was just the seams that were leaking, but at closer inspection, the water was actually seeping through the fabric.

In the morning, everything was soaked, and by eight o'clock the sun was shining on the rocks around camp so I was able to lay everything out to dry. It was the perfect time to go fishing. Within minutes, I was off to fish and explore Rose Lake.

By the time I arrived at the lake, the sun was high enough to illuminate the deep water along the edge of the lake. What a magnificent lake, the mountains surrounding it like an amphitheater. I only wish the fishing was as good as the view. After two hours of exploring the south side of the lake, I only hooked two nine-inch fish. Both were golden trout, coaxed by a yellow-bodied Stimulator.

On the way back to camp, I fished the outlet stream through the meadow and landed eight fish to eight inches. The outlet stream gradually tumbled down through a grassy hillside strewn with boulders and a few clumps of willow bushes. It was easy and entertaining fishing. Mac found this stream to be "fairly swarmed with golden trout running larger than I had ever seen in streams before."

The author at Rose Lake

Charles McDermand at Rose Lake, circa 1945

Once at camp, I found that most of my gear was dry and only needed to be flipped to finish drying the undersides.

Taka and his camp mate suffered far worse than me. Halfway through the night they realized they pitched their tents in the low-lying area, and they awoke to a flooded sleeping area. They were still trying to dry their equipment in the meadow when I left my camp for the trail. That was the last time I saw Taka, unfortunately, and we never crossed paths again.

I decided to forego fishing Marie Lake, as Mac says it was fishless and the rain and hail had returned. I was also intent on getting over Seldon Pass to camp for the night.

Mac had prospected the lakes between Heart Lake and Seldon Pass with Lefty, his hiking buddy. With the rain and hail still an issue, I reluctantly chose to skip that adventure and leave it for another trip, but when I got to Heart Lake, the rain had slowed to a drizzle. Now was my chance, I thought. I rigged my rod, climbed down to the water's edge, and cast from a prominent rock. My first two casts brought a rise with each retrieval. Then it began to pour again and I was forced off the lake. I needed to get to a camp, pitch the tarp, and pray that it would hold up and not leak too much.

* * *

I made it to Sallie Keyes Lakes in a fine mist of rain, just enough to make it annoying. I pitched the tarp between two big trees, gathered enough dry firewood (even though I was 200 feet above the fire restriction zone), and I hunkered in until the rain stopped.

Each time the rain stopped, I would jump out with my rod and fish. All the fish I caught were golden trout and I took them on a variety of dry flies (yellow Humpy, small Royal Wolf, and Stimulator). During the breaks in the rain showers, I worked my way to the inlet stream that led to the upper lake. There, at about seven o'clock in the evening, I had about forty-five minutes of pure pleasure. I took one cast after another, landing a fish nearly every cast. I had my limit of five in the first six casts.

As an experiment, I switched to a series of wet flies. I was skunked with the wet flies. Not a single strike! All of the fish were golden trout and each had a different set of markings and colorations. I kept my limit of five to present to Dad tomorrow at Florence Lake for dinner. I knew that he would be happy to have fresh trout.

There was a hunting party camped not far from me between the two lakes. I talked to them while they fished for their dinner. Three of them were casting sinkers and power bait into the lower lake. We talked about deer hunting, fishing, and this beautiful area. They were hay growers from the San Joaquin

Valley, and each year they would strike a deal with the local horse packer to pack them up here to hunt in exchange for providing hay for the packer's stock. Oddly, they all did not look like the typical archery deer hunters. These guys were older, out of shape, and not quite so stealthy in their movements in the woods. Maybe it was the whiskey?

Sallie Keyes limit

With nearly 3,000 feet to descend, I was up early and broke camp by 7:15 in the morning. The air was cool and damp as I walked along the trail where it followed the edge of the lower lake. I stopped to talk with the hunters as they cooked their breakfast of bacon and eggs. It smelled so good; I just wanted to stay there on the trail to inhale the smells for a while.

Nearing the head of Florence Lake, I passed a family on the trail. First in line was a young girl, about fifteen years old. I asked her if she came in on the eleven o'clock ferry and she replied yes, barely stopping as she focused on the trail. Next, I ran into what had to have been her younger brother, maybe twelve years old, and I asked him where they were headed. His reply was a very matter-of-fact "up." I chuckled under my breath and told him that he was headed in the right direction. Soon, I crossed paths with their parents. I stopped briefly to talk and found out they were from Scotts Valley, only several miles from where I live.

I arrived at Florence Lake at 11:30 with plenty of time to fish along the granite shoreline, swim, take a quick bath, and enjoy the company of two guys coming out of the wilderness after a short backpack trip. The ferry arrived at one o'clock, and after a short boat ride we were at the store near the dam at the end of the road.

When I got to the store, Dad wasn't there. We had pre-determined that I might arrive at the store either the afternoon of August 23rd or the morning of the next day. I was early and enjoyed the opportunity to sit and relax while sipping on an ice cold Coke. Dad arrived about three hours later, and we drove to Jackass Campground and settled in for the evening.

With almost eight decades of life behind him, Dad is still spry and spirited. His excitement surrounding the Sierra Nevada is truly infectious. If he was not pointing out wildflowers, he was listening to and enjoying the songs of the mountain chickadees. We enjoyed our evenings, talking about fishing, past trips, and backpacking traditions. One tradition that we talked about was his preferred reading material while in the backcountry. He always carried his copy of *Sierra Nevada Natural History: An Illustrated Handbook* by Tracy Storer and Robert Usinger. He has always been a student of the plants and animals of the Sierra Nevada. Dad could recite the names of most of the trees and shrubs, the birds (even while on wing), the voice of a pica, or the identity of the wildflowers in the meadows. I have his copy and frequently use it as a reference. Dad had forgotten about that book and didn't remember that it was full of his notes and comments strewn throughout its dog-eared and faded pages.

As a kid, I always thought my father knew everything about everything. It would always amaze me that when asked a question, he never faltered in providing an intelligent answer with extreme confidence. He laughed when I told him that I thought he was the smartest man I knew. It wasn't until my early adult years when my sister, Tammi, pointed out that with him it was either "fact or fiction." He has the ability of answering a question or making a statement with such conviction that even with completely false and factless information, we would believe him. The night was full of jokes, stories and memories.

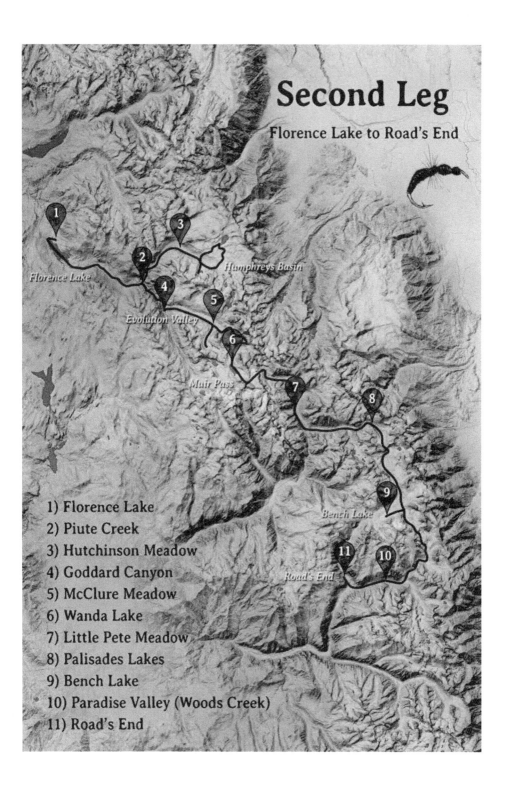

Second Leg

Florence Lake to Road's End

Florence Lake

Humphreys Basin

Evolution Valley

Muir Pass

Bench Lake

Road's End

1) Florence Lake
2) Piute Creek
3) Hutchinson Meadow
4) Goddard Canyon
5) McClure Meadow
6) Wanda Lake
7) Little Pete Meadow
8) Palisades Lakes
9) Bench Lake
10) Paradise Valley (Woods Creek)
11) Road's End

CHAPTER 4

Florence Lake to Evolution Lake

Ten Best Fishing Spots in the Sierras
(not in order)

1. *Piute Creek—pool after pool of goldens*
2. *Thousand Island Lake—big fish*
3. *Upper Le Conte Canyon, Middle Fork of the Kings River—goldens to ten inches*
4. *Little Kern River—goldens to thirteen inches*
5. *Bench Lake—browns to fifteen inches*
6. *Silver Lake—steelheads to fifteen inches*
7. *Heidi Lake—full of ten- to twelve-inch brookies eager to take my flies*
8. *Lake of the Lone Indian—fish to twelve inches*
9. *Virginia Lake—big brookies and goldens*
10. *Mono Creek—big pools and fast, clear water with browns, brookies, and rainbows*

Even though Dad would rather be hiking with me, his knee would not allow that to happen. Home cooked food, ice-cold beer, and a two-day visit would have to do. As it turns out, it was exactly what I needed. Thanks, Dad. You are one of the rocks in my life.

Dad and I spent the day getting my gear straight (he brought my next food drop that would last me another two weeks), eating some fantastic food, and setting out to find cell phone coverage to call our wives. We hiked and fished the South Fork of the San Joaquin River below the Florence Lake Dam, where I had a few strikes but didn't land any fish.

My brother, Scott, and his son, Nicholas, arrived in mid-afternoon in a whirlwind of activity to get their gear, food, and minds ready for six days on the trail with me. We spread out all of their gear and food items on two picnic tables at the campsite. Despite absolutely no organization on their end prior to their arrival, we had their packs organized, fishing gear and tackle ready, all before darkness arrived. Scott also brought me a new, ultra-light rain fly to replace my old leaky one. It was so great to be here in the Sierra with Dad, Scott, and Nicholas. We sat around the fire at night and reminisced about many of the family backpack trips.

I spent over a year preparing for this trip, spending countless hours reading Mac's books and articles, studying maps, preparing gear and food lists, and working to get into shape. I wanted to do most of the hike solo, but also tried to coordinate with others to hike different sections with me. Mac often hiked solo, but seemed to enjoy hiking with various partners during his many trips into the Sierra Nevada. He often hiked with his good friend Lefty, however, Mac provides the reader very little information about Lefty's true identity. Vic, another hiking buddy, was formally Frank Victor Novacek (born May 19, 1919). Mac's second book, *Yosemite and Kings Canyon Trout*, allowed the reader a closer look at his hiking partners. The multiple trips that he took in the years following 1945 became the basis for his second book. Most hikes were completed with an assortment of other partners, including Breckenridge, Cousin Merl, John Tarkington, Coastguardsman Joe Corbett of Austin Texas, "Speedy" Marable, Jim Anderson, Kimberly, the deer hunter, Les Carlson and his wife Millie, and Johnny Messner. On one trip, Mac also backpacked with Helen, his wife.

It was so great of Dad to keep us fed with some amazing home-cooked food. He brought pork *verde*, T-bone steaks, fettuccine with Alfredo sauce, egg and cheese muffins, watermelon, banana nut bread, and peaches and cream for dessert. The ice-cold beer was the best!

Breakfast, several cups of mocha, and a roaring fire did a great job of setting our minds straight. Dad played the role of a gracious host and helped us get our stuff together and our cars shuttled around before we caught the ferry across the lake to the trailhead. I could see that dad was fighting back his emotions and wished that he could join us. After sending us off, he had a bit of a drive to get back to his home in Ojai.

Scott, Nicholas, and I caught the 10:30 ferry to the other side of the lake and back to the John Muir Trail. This spared us an extra four and a half miles of hiking. We traversed the eight miles up to Piute Creek with little challenge, set up camp, and set off to fish Piute Creek and the South Fork of the San Joaquin River.

Florence Lake send off

My fondest memory of Piute Creek was from my family's 1968 backpacking trip, when we went from South Lake (on the east side of the Sierra) and looped around to North Lake (not far from South Lake). We stopped at Piute Creek for lunch under a big pine tree on the south side of the bridge. I remember working my way upstream and fishing each pool. As the water cascaded over each rocky ledge and into the next pool, the fishing was near perfect. I could easily sneak up to a pool from below and make a short cast into the pool above. It seemed that every cast netted a fish. They were all small, but it was exciting. What more could any seven-year-old kid want?

Scott lands a small rainbow

Scott with a big golden from above Big Pete Meadow, 1968

Author's sister, Tammi, with catch, circa 1968

Scott, Nicholas, and I worked our way down Piute Creek, fishing each hole that provided fishable water. The creek was running fast and the banks were frequently choked with brush, making it a challenge to get to the water and cast without fouling our lines. Within the first quarter mile of the stream, Nicholas lost several flies and nearly lost the tip of his rod. He walked back to camp soaked to his waist after having to go in after his gear. He happened to be tying his knots wrong and kept flipping his flies off his leader as he casted. After a quick knot-tying tutorial, we were off to explore again.

All but one of the fish we caught on the lower Piute and a half-mile of the South Fork of the San Joaquin River were rainbows or rainbow-golden hybrids. Scott brought in a very skinny ten-and-a-half-inch brown trout. Scott and Nicholas each landed three fish and lost many more. I was able to land a total of six fish to ten inches. The most productive flies were grasshoppers, a Royal Coachman, a yellow-bodied Stimulator, and a red-bodied Humpy. I tried a rust-colored, bead-headed leech in some of the bigger pools, with no luck. When we could get to a pocket of water, the fish seemed very interested in all of our offerings.

With a 1,500-foot elevation climb to Hutchinson Meadow, we made our way up the trail as it followed alongside Piute Creek. I was looking forward to a quiet section of trail with few other backpackers once we separated from the John Muir Trail. Not so. It happened to be part of the route that backpackers hike while doing the South Lake to North Lake Loop—the very same loop we did in 1968, now a popular route. We passed a number of backpackers along the way.

We stopped to fish Piute Creek where it meets the trail. There were big, beautiful pools, each at the base of a series of small cataracts. In thirty minutes, we landed seventeen fish. All were less than nine inches long and most were golden, with a few brookies. In one pool alone, I took nine fish. Surprisingly, the fish didn't seem to spook too easily. The water was so clear and serene I could see dozens of active fish in each pocket of water.

Prime fishing at Piute Creek

The route that Mac took with his hiking partner, Vic, up this very same trail brought them up into French Canyon and over Pine Creek Pass. They fished the lakes on the other side of the pass, including Pine Lake, Upper Pine Lake, and Honeymoon Lake. They did well in those lakes, and were rewarded with some big fish. If we were going to follow that route, we would not have the opportunity to visit the Evolution Valley area, since we had only a few days to fish and hike together. We opted to skip that section.

We planned to spend the afternoon fishing the creek and lakes in the French Canyon basin and not to go up and over Pine Creek Pass. Once we got to Hutchinson Meadow, it was too late in the afternoon to fish anything other than the creek in French Canyon. Looking at the map, we had set up camp only half a mile away from the trail to Lower Honeymoon Lake, and decided to make the 1,000-foot climb to fish it and explore that area for the afternoon. The trail went up the side of the canyon and was not very well marked or maintained. At times, the faint trail went straight uphill without switchbacks.

Lower Honeymoon Lake

We fished all the way around the lake and caught only goldens to eight inches. Dry flies worked the best (Hoppers, Royal Coachman, and yellow Humpy). On the way back, we fished Piute Creek with dry flies and hooked too many small goldens and brookies to count. We did keep a few of the larger fish for dinner.

With a lunch packed, we set off the next morning to fish

Humphreys Basin for the day and headed up the trail toward Piute Pass. About three miles up the trail, we all commented on how the trail kept taking off uphill in a series of switchbacks for no apparent reason. We cursed the trail crew for their seemingly poor judgment in trail route planning. Consulting the map, we decided to head cross country to Tomahawk Lake, then circle around to fish the other lakes, rather than follow the wandering trail.

From the top of the ridge, we had a commanding view of the entire Humphreys Basin, including Glacier Divide. We climbed up onto a prominent rock to take a few pictures and admire the view.

Glacier Divide from Humphreys Basin

Tomahawk Lake produced a nice twelve-and-a-half-inch brookie that nabbed Nicholas' fly near a submerged rock. He offered an ugly green-bodied and brown-hackled fly with a red tail. The fly really didn't resemble any insect that I have seen. I landed one small brookie with a Stimulator while Scott got skunked.

Nicholas's thirteen-inch brookie from Tomahawk Lake

"The Pose," Glacier Divide from Humphreys Basin

A man camped on the north side of the lake said that he

pulled four sixteen-inchers out of Tomahawk Lake using power bait. He also said that his horse packer had caught a nineteen-inch golden trout out of Mesa Lake a few days prior. So, with big fish on our minds, we set off cross country again to Mesa Lake. We fished halfway around the lake and found no fish—not even a sign of fish. Discouraged, we became eager to see if the big trout that Mac found in Desolation Lake were still there. Along the way, we wet our flies in tiny Wedge Lake. It was more of a lakelet that didn't seem to be able to harbor fish because of its small size and shallow depth.

We arrived at Desolation Lake in time for lunch. The wind at times was stiff and cool, which made it harder to cast our flies to where we wanted. Again we found no fish or sign of fish. All three of us must have changed flies a dozen times in an attempt to find the right combination. This was a big lake with a lot of shoreline, and we could have easily spent several days exploring the entire lake to find the right fly to bring up the big fish. When Mac visited Desolation Lake in 1944, he found it full of big fish. Oddly, the fish would not hit any of the flies he presented, either.

On our way down to Lower Desolation Lake, Nicholas spotted an animal running away from us in the distance. His first thought was that it was a fox, given its gait and long white tail. When it took off running again, we all concluded that it was a jackrabbit—the big ears were unmistakable. It was a *big* jackrabbit. Ten minutes later, we saw another one only ten yards from where we stood. He had a long, fluffy white tail, and stood taller than any other jackrabbit we had ever seen. He sat still long enough for me to get a few pictures. Having had enough with us, he ran away again with the most unusual gait, running like a dog with a hop every once in a while. As it turns out, he was a white-tailed jackrabbit, the largest of all hares and quite rare in the Sierra.

Lower Desolation Lake provided only a few strikes for us, with no fish landed. We saw a few cruisers along the shoreline as we skirted the lake. The term "cruiser" is what I use to describe a fish that slowly swims near the shore of the lake, seemingly cruising along in search for food.

This trip would not be complete if we passed up Golden Trout Lakes. So, with daylight limited, we decided to visit just the lower lake. Scott caught the only fish at Lower Golden Trout Lake. He used a Royal Coachman to entice the lone fish, a small brookie. That's right—a brook trout in Golden Trout Lake. Go figure.

White-tailed jackrabbit in Humphreys Basin

We followed the outlet creek from Golden Trout Lake (Piute Creek) back toward camp, at times walking on the "old" trail. It seemed to be a better, more direct trail than the "new" existing one. This section of creek produced goldens and brookies to ten inches, using Royal Coachman, black and white

Stimulator, and grasshopper dry flies.

The three of us worked well together to get a big fire roaring, clean our fish for dinner, and put together another fine feast. This time we cooked our fish with corn meal, bacon, and a little wild parsley that Nicholas had foraged.

* * *

Descending down the canyon was a treat. Having just come up the trail two days prior, we knew what to expect. Nicholas couldn't figure out why it was easier going down the canyon than it was going up. The easy stroll up the South Fork of the San Joaquin River was quite picturesque, and I found myself eyeing each pool and wanting to stop and explore each one.

We found a good campsite in Goddard Canyon at Evolution Creek, just up from the junction of the John Muir Trail. Our intention was to get away from the crowds on the trail, as the campsites in the area were filling up fast. With plenty of afternoon left, we hiked up to where Evolution Creek falls out of the canyon above. There was a magnificent pool at the base of a grand fall, and all of us pulled a fish or two out of the turquoise-colored treasure. Mac talks about fishing that very same pool where he "hooked and released several small golden trout and one eleven-inch scrapper that looked like the colored plate of the Kern River Gilbert rainbow—a husky fellow with a profusion of black spots and a vivid crimson lateral band."

We attempted to fish the rest of Evolution Creek below the falls, but our attempts were thwarted by massive amounts of brush that made it nearly impossible to even get close to the water, let alone have enough room for any sort of cast. Giving up, we decided to walk down the John Muir Trail to where it comes close to the South Fork of the San Joaquin River. All the fish, except one rainbow, were golden trout. None were over nine inches, and we used grasshoppers, green-bodied Stimulator, a black Woolly Bugger, and Royal Coachman flies.

As we ascended the trail toward Evolution Valley the next morning, we could not help ourselves. We had to stop and fish the majestic pools created by the creek as it cascades down the canyon wall toward the South Fork of the San Joaquin River. Each pool teemed with small golden trout. Some pools were difficult to get to and required a fair amount of skill to climb down the rock faces. Most pools were brilliant colors of green, blue, and aqua—very inviting to any fly angler willing to make the effort.

Scott, Evolution Creek Falls

As we entered McClure Meadow, we found the same campsite that we as a family had camped at in 1968. One memorable photograph from that trip is of my brothers, Scott and Eric, and me in the creek next to the meadow. We were in our underwear, the Hermit in the background, and we were splashing about in the water. So we attempted to re-create the picture, with Nicholas as a stand-in for Eric. After the laughs and a bit of reflection, we just sat there in the grass next to the creek for about an hour, soaking in the sights. This is truly one of my favorite places in the Sierra Nevada.

Colby Meadow, 1968

Just above the Ranger's Cabin at McClure Meadow, we stumbled upon the campsite next to the "rock slide" where our Boy Scout troop, Troop 236, camped in 1972. My brothers and I were all Eagle Scouts and belonged to the same troop in Danville, California. Every year our troop would complete a fifty-mile backpack trip. I was so excited to find this place again that I didn't notice a hiker sitting on a rock next to the creek eating his lunch. After apologies for interrupting his lunch, we took pictures and talked about what we remembered from that trip. I just had to get a picture of me fishing from a rock in the middle of the creek. It was the same rock I was standing on in 1972, when a picture of me was taken while I attempted to extricate my fly out of the tree overhanging the creek.

Todd catching trees at slide rock hole during 1972 Scout trip

After a bit of searching, we found a good area to make camp next to Evolution Creek near its confluence with McGee Creek. Nicholas wanted to hang out around camp and relax awhile, so Scott and I hiked to McGee Lakes. We took off cross country while keeping the Hermit on our left. A short way up the hillside, we ran into an old trail and followed it all the way to the lakes. At times, we would lose the trail, only to find it again after a short search for the next duck. (A duck is a set of three rocks stacked on top of each other to assist hikers with finding the route). Scott kept saying he felt we had been there before. I didn't think so and we bantered back and forth for a while about who had a better memory. When I got back home after my trip, I found the 1958 topographic map that I had (the same map we used on our 1968 trip) and it did show that there was an official trail. To top that, there was a dotted red line drawn on the map to show the route we took during that trip. The line extended all the way up to McGee Lakes and back. So, as it turns out, Scott has the better memory on that point. We *were* there in 1968. The current map, however, does not show that a trail to the lakes exists. Apparently the park service has abandoned the trail officially.

Scott, Eric, and Todd swimming – Evolution Valley, 1968

Todd and Scott swimming—and missing Eric, Evolution Valley

McGee Lakes harbored a healthy population of golden trout. Mac visited these lakes twice, and both times thought them to be fishless. Mac writes, "These deep, picturesque bodies of water were fishless as far as I could see. Disappointed, I walked clear around one of them to make certain. However, it is possible that the trout had merely withdrawn to the depths. Two different parties have since told me that these lakes contain trout. I hope so, for here it seemed to me would be another natural home of *Salmo roseveltii*."

We caught lanky golden trout that all seemed to have their own unique variations and color patterns. Some fish were *very* bright (like the fish in the outlet stream), while others were either dull or devoid of their parr marks. Dry flies seemed to work best. The fish we caught were all under nine inches in length. I tried two wet flies (a white Muddler with a red stripe and the rust-colored, bead-headed streamer). They produced a ton of followers, but only a few strikes.

McGee Creek

We found the upper lake to be very deep, with lots of cruisers to ten or eleven inches. Where the creek between the two lakes drains into the lower lake, the fish were rising all over the place. They weren't too interested in the flies we were offering, so we headed back to camp.

Scott and I found Nicholas sitting next to a roaring fire, ready for dinner. He'd had a relaxing afternoon fishing and soaking his feet in the creek. Nicholas is quite a skilled cook and had put together a delicious dinner. All he needed was our McGee Lake fish to complete the spread.

Sunset at camp on Evolution Creek

* * *

For the last six days, I have had the great fortune to be in the company of Scott and Nicholas. There is a *very* short list of people that I would invite to join me on a segment of this trek. Their enthusiasm for fishing, advanced backpacking abilities, and desire to keep my goals in focus made for a perfect combination.

I had decided to skip a visit to the Darwin Lakes area. It would take a few days to explore the lakes and feeder creeks properly. Mac visited the lakes in 1945 and found the travel very steep and rugged. He did it with his pack, another testament to his gritty athletic abilities, and found them to be a picture of cold sterility. In another lake he found a ten-inch "sleek specimen of the most beautiful trout that swims. He dangled a vivid chaos of color: blood red, cream, ivory tan, jet black, and orange." He found some lakes with frogs and pollywogs and others with no fish. A stewpan full of goldens from one lake was carefully carried to another lake during his trip in an attempt to populate the sterile lake with goldens. I would like to visit these lakes in the future, and would be interested to see if, after seventy years, fish have survived.

The 1968 family trip allowed us to explore the Darwin Lakes area as well. The few pictures from that trip show that we had great fishing success with some big fish. Mom and Dad, once again, got all of us kids up those steep granite slopes to another out-of-the-way bit of paradise.

In typical Scott Bruce fashion, he wanted to climb the granite knoll just north of Evolution Lake (for photographic reasons, he pleaded). We were all glad we did. The view down the Evolution Valley and of the surrounding mountains was magnificent. Straight ahead of us was The Hermit. From our vantage point, it was a jagged, sharp-topped peak, vastly different from its appearance from the valley floor, where it is distinctly dome-shaped with smooth sides.

Directly behind us was Mount Darwin, magnificent Mount Darwin. This is truly rugged, desolate, and formidable country. I love it here and cannot describe the flood of emotions that overtook me.

In 1895, Theodore S. Solomons, a charter member of the Sierra Club, was on an expedition through this area. He was determined to find a north to south route close to the Sierra crest, which in time would be called the John Muir Trail. In Francis Farquar's *History of the Sierra Nevada*, he says the following of the explorer: "To these peaks, Solomons gave the names of philosophers in whose theories he was interested—Darwin, Huxley, Haeckel, Spencer, Wallace, and Fisk—the 'Evolution Group.'" Evolution Valley and Evolution Lake were later named after this group of philosophers.

We fished Evolution Lake and found only a few small golden trout. I had a few strikes, but Scott caught two eight-inchers and a small four-inch beauty. Dry flies received the only action. All of us switched flies numerous times in an attempt to find what worked best. It was a bit windy, so we had to adjust our casting strategies in order to get our flies where we thought the fish would be hiding.

View of Evolution Valley

Scott and I found the exact spot where Mac stood to take the picture of Evolution Lake that is printed in his book. We were amazed at how little the trees across the lake had grown in seventy years. The trees are a little taller now, yet still stunted. Not much else had changed over the years.

It was sad to see Scott and Nicholas leave, and was a bit emotional for me. We had a great time reminiscing about our backpacking trips and about growing up in the Bruce household. We talked a lot about how awesome it was to see Dad at Florence Lake and how much we missed Mom. Together, they did a great job raising us and giving us the opportunities to grow and be who we are today.

Evolution Lake, 1945

*Evolution Lake, 2012, taken from same spot
where Mac took his picture in 1945*

CHAPTER 5

Evolution Lake to Little Pete Meadow

My focus changed to the hike to Sapphire Lake. Once there, I planned to camp and then hike to the unnamed lakes above to fish and explore. When I got to Sapphire Lake, it was quite windy, but I found a spot to camp that was mildly blocked by the prevailing wind. It would work, but it was not ideal.

It was an incredible climb up and over a massive boulder field to get to the small lakes above Sapphire Lake. It was a challenge to hop and climb from one boulder to another. Every time I clambered onto a boulder, I hoped that the rock would be secure and not topple over. All three small puddles above Sapphire Lake were a disappointment, with no sign of fish. What a waste of time and energy from a fishing standpoint!

Back at Sapphire Lake, the wind continued to blow hard, so I packed up and headed to Wanda Lake, 11,426 feet above sea level. A nook in the rocks above the trail and out of the wind made for a perfect camp. Between the clouds, the sun was shining on Muir Pass as it sank into the horizon behind the mountains. I could see the Muir Hut at the top of the pass from the edge of the lake near my campsite. From the planning phase of the trip up until this point, getting to the hut, for me, had been the most anticipated part of the trip.

Eric with catch from nearby Darwin Lake, 1968

My campsite up in the rocks and away from the water proved to be the coldest night yet. The moon was full and I woke to a fair amount of frosted dew on my sleeping bag and gear. It was also the quietest, with not a sound all night.

I was packed up and out of camp faster than ever before. As I walked along the edge of Wanda Lake, I took the opportunity to make a few casts and try a few fly patterns. I saw no fish and had no strikes. Wanda does appear fishless even though it is very deep and looks as though it could support a healthy fish population. Mac made no mention of the fishing at Wanda Lake when he visited in 1945.

Wanda Lake, looking at Muir Pass during sunset

Wanda Lake from Muir Pass, 1968

Leaving Wanda Lake behind, I pushed ahead for Lake McDermand. This lake, named after Charles McDermand, sits about three hundred yards off the trail, so I dropped my pack and set off over a field of boulders to the lake. As I approached it, I saw a lone seagull floating on the lake near a prime fishing rock along the shoreline. How odd, I thought. He was the only gull I saw the entire trip. He seemed out of place, too far from the ocean and too high in elevation for a gull's normal range.

I had three strikes on the first three casts using a big red Humpy with white wings. As I continued to work the fly in that area, finding no more action, I moved along the shore and switched flies. Interestingly, when I moved, the gull took flight in the stiff breeze and landed just offshore from where I set up to fish again. He followed me two more times as I moved and switched flies, presumably doing his own fishing. I tried three different leech patterns, a grasshopper, and then went back to the red Humpy, but to no avail.

Lake McDermand

The gull finally gave up and flew off just as it began to rain and hail. Was the gull's presence and movements a sign? Who knows! In 1960, two of Mac's friends (Les Sadler of Stinson Beach, California, and Ed Neal, a staff writer for the *San Francisco Examiner & Chronicle,* backpacked to this lake to fish for golden trout. Mac had intended to accompany them, however, a week prior, he had suffered his first stroke. They fished Lake McDermand (it was unnamed then) for only thirty minutes. In that time, they landed six full-bodied goldens from eleven to thirteen inches and lost many more.

The rain and hail was my sign that I needed to get a move on and get to the hut. It seemed almost cold enough to snow.

In 1968, when I was here last, this small tarn was still unnamed on the maps, and we walked past it without giving it so much as a glance. It wasn't until after I returned from this trip that I learned how this lake was named and who was the driving force behind the process. The US Geological Survey has the authority to oversee the process of naming features. The US Board on Geographic Names has the responsibility and makes all decisions based on several criteria. They first attempt to use local names when possible and most were assigned many years ago when the first surveys and mapping outings occurred in the late 1800s. The process is the same regardless of jurisdiction. A proposal to name a feature can be suggested through an application process. If those who have jurisdiction approve and there are no objections, the name is then appointed. Some of the criteria for naming features after individuals include the following: No natural feature may be named for a living person, the person must have been deceased at least five years, the person must have a direct and long term association with the feature, and the person must have made notable civic contributions.

Lake McDermand was proposed in 1967 by the officers and staff of the Department Store Employee's Union Local 1100 in

San Francisco (Mac's last employer). The application was signed by Mr. Walt Johnson and advanced by friends and fishing buddies Joe Wampler, Max Wolff, L.E. (Spud) Lewis, Dwight Strong, Les Sadler, and Ed Neal of the *San Francisco Sunday Examiner & Chronicle*. This lake was chosen because it was a fitting "lonely panorama among the nude mountains and harboring a pure strain of golden trout," as written by Ed Neal on December 10, 1967, in the *San Francisco Sunday Examiner & Chronicle*. The verdict was published in Decision List 6704 and the entry reads as follows:

> *McDermand, Lake, 0.3 miles long, elevation 11,548, in Kings Canyon National Park, 0.3 miles east of Wanda Lake and 2.5 miles northeast of Mount Goddard; named for Charles K. McDermand (1902 - 1966), outdoorsman, writer, and authority on golden trout fishing in the High Sierra; Fresno Co., California; 37'07'05" N, 118'40' 50" W.*

The individuals responsible for making this happen had planned to erect a simple rock cairn and plaque at the lake in honor of Mac. The plaque was apparently designed by one of Mac's protégés, artist Nick Pendleton, and was to be erected the summer of 1968. I am not sure if this happened or not. When I visited the lake on my trip, I did not see any sort of plaque or memorial. It is possible that I missed it as I was pushed away by the approaching storm. It is more probable that a memorial was erected and then subsequently removed. A few years ago, the national park forbade this sort of signage within the park's boundary.

As I walked away from Lake McDermand, I could not get the gull out of my mind. Mac was a great fisherman and a fine spokesman for golden trout. I honestly feel that the bird's presence was some sort of sign. What that sign was, I am not sure. Either way, my visit was a collision of many emotions and experiences that made me honored to be at Mac's namesake lake.

* * *

When I made it to the hut, there were five other hikers inside trying to keep warm and shelter themselves from the storm. One hiker was making coffee while another was making breakfast on their stoves. During a pause in the rain, I ran across the hillside to the only snow patch on the pass with my Sierra cup. I made a cherry snow cone (using cherry-flavored Kool-Aid sprinkled over the snow) and talked with the other hikers until the rain stopped. A backpack trip in the Sierra would not be complete without a snow cone. It is the Bruce way! We grew up always searching for the closest snow patch. Snow cones, a snowball fight, or just skiing on the soles of our boots was a break we always looked forward to.

Family snow cone break, circa 1969

Scott remembers our visit to the Muir Hut well. He recalls dropping our packs with a hurried excitement and scrambling over to a nearby snow patch just before we climbed the highest pass we had ever been over. We filled all of our sierra cups with snow so we could enjoy a fruit-flavored snow cone inside the hut.

The hut was just as I had remembered: stone construction (just like one would build an igloo) with a dome-shaped roof and a wooden Dutch door. The fireplace has since been filled with rocks to prevent it from being used. Apparently, with no wood around, the National Park Service wants to deter its use and keep the dead wood on the ground for the plants and animals. There were still a few sticks of kindling beneath one bench. A sign next to the door asks guests not to leave anything in the hut—pack it in, pack it out.

In his book in 1945, Mac recalled, "At Evolution Lake, which is the last source of fuel before reaching the pass, a large sign requests pack trains to carry a few sticks of firewood to the Muir Hut to be stored in case of emergency." That practice of stocking fuel for emergency fires, and the sign indicating so, are long gone.

Dad remembers our 1968 hut experience differently: We had stopped there briefly for lunch, thinking that Wanda Lake was just before we went over Muir Pass at the upper end of Evolution Valley. He thinks we didn't have time to fish because the weather was starting to close in. By the time we got to the stone hut, he remembers that it was snowing steadily. With the hut jammed with people, all smelling terrible, Mom wouldn't even stick her head inside. We moved on, wanting to get down below the snow level so we could camp by ourselves. At times, he thought, it was hard to find the trail as the snow continued to build up. Since it was getting late, we found a small level spot off the trail and set up our tarp and climbed in with just snacks— he didn't remember building a fire that night. We camped right at the snow level where it was very wet, and by morning our sleeping bags were soaked. We rang them out, packed up, and headed down into Le Conte Canyon as soon as the sun came out the next morning. Later in the day, we found a nice camping spot, rested, dried out our sleeping bags, and ate a great meal.

Muir Hut, 1968 (Author in middle)

My memories of the hut are different. Certainly, the pictures show a warm sunny day. One photograph shows all of us inside the hut sitting next to the fireplace. I do remember seeing a stack of canned food left behind by other hikers to be used in an emergency. Either way, being back was memorable.

Inside the Muir Hut, 1968 (Author at bottom left)

Muir Hut, present day

The skies parted and I hiked down the trail to Helen Lake after saying goodbye to the hikers in the hut. I stopped twice to fish and survey the lake, but saw no sign of fish. Mac found a great school of thick-bodied, rose-colored fish with black spots on their shoulders that were endowed with small heads and tails. He said they had resembled small salmon. The fish schooled at the outlet, where it was illegal to fish back in 1945, so he never caught any.

Helen Lake

Down the trail from Helen Lake are three unnamed lakes. The first lake appeared to have no sign of life, the second lake was full of frogs and pollywogs, and the third was again fishless, shallow, and mossy. I fished several pools in the stream below the third lake and caught nothing. I have since found out that these lakes were part of the Sierra yellow-legged frog reintroduction program of the California Department of Fish and Wildlife. They sterilized the lakes to kill off all the fish, then planted them with frog eggs.

Helen Lake marmot

There is a point where the trail came close to the creek (Middle Fork of Kings River) and made a good resting and fishing spot. The creek upstream from the camp was a beautiful cascade of pools, perfect for easy casting. An unusually decorated rock caught my attention as I walked along the trail. A slice of a large boulder facing the campsite had fallen to the ground. Over the years, people have added other rocks in strategic places to give it eyes and teeth, creating a monster. I feel like I remember this from past trips, or maybe I have seen a picture of it somewhere. I had an odd *déjà vu* while I was there.

It is possible that the monster was here in 1968 when I passed through on a trip with my family.

Monster Rock

Almost immediately I caught two eleven-inch golden trout out of the pools in the creek. I lost the first one when I bent down to grab it out of the pool next to the swifter water. I slipped on a rock, did that shuffle-dance thing common with fishermen trying to stand or walk on slippery rocks, and then stepped into the water up to my knee. In all the commotion, the fish managed to dislodge the fly and flip away. I even stood up and looked around self-consciously to be sure there was no one around to witness such a comical event.

Turning to the next pool with a wet left foot, and paying closer attention to the slippery rocks, I firmly hooked another eleven-incher. Both fish fought hard and were some of the brightest colored fish I'd seen thus far, with brilliant oranges, reds, and olive colors on their backs.

Just below Big Pete Meadow, I stopped to fish the pools

at the base of a series of extensive cataracts. As my sleeping bag and wet sock dried in the sun on the rocks above, I caught one fish after another. All of them were golden trout and between eight and eleven inches in length. I was entertained by the fish in the pool at the base of a significant cascade as I watched them trying to jump the whitewater and swim up the falls. About every two minutes, one would make an attempt with a grand jump, only to get flung back into the pool where it started. I can't imagine any fish being able to make that leap, but they still tried, driven by instinct.

Le Conte Canyon and the upper portions of the Middle Fork of the Kings River are a solid fishing experience, one of the best of the Sierra for me. The golden trout are larger—up to twelve inches—vibrant, and strong fighters.

I made camp downstream from Little Pete Meadow and across the river, settling in for a very peaceful night with a fire and fish dinner. The area around the trail junction to Dusy Basin and Bishop Pass was busy and crowded, and I just wanted some peace and quiet.

*Bright golden from Middle Fork of the Kings River
above Big Pete Meadow, near Monster Rock*

View of Little Pete Meadow

Family in rain gear looking down into Little Pete Meadow, 1968

A fire brought the day's adventures into focus. So many nights growing up backpacking were spent together by a fire, almost as a ritual. Mom used to tell "Shaggy Dog" stories. They were usually run-on stories that she would tell off the top of her head, making it up as she went along. All had a plot, were very captivating for us, and usually had a hanging ending that left us wanting more.

My mother, Barbara (Chase) Bruce, was an amazing individual. She died at age fifty-five of heart disease, which was a shock to all who know her. Besides being an extremely capable outdoor enthusiast, she was a very talented artist. Her creativity was varied and spread across just about any medium that she touched. Whether as a painter, actress, seamstress, athlete, or a mentor, she touched many people and was always there for her family. Much of who I am is because of her, and she is, in part, a big reason for me taking the trip.

CHAPTER 6

Little Pete Meadow to Bench Lake

I was back on the trail the next morning. Next along the trail was Grouse Meadow. I walked out into the meadow from a well-developed campsite next to the trail. The grass in the shade was still covered in frost from the night before. The river meandered slowly through the meadow, a twisting ribbon of water as it glides around the big boulders. Standing on the grassy bank, I casted to dozens of small goldens as they swam about, looking for the little bugs that danced on top of the water. The water in the river moves so slowly that it makes no sound. As I fished, I heard a duck quacking somewhere downriver. A single bird noisily looked for its mate. A few other birds called in the distance, yet it was so quiet that I could hear the trout slurp and splash as they rose to the surface for a snack. All up and down the river, the fish were making dimples on the water.

Mac's route took a wrong turn on his trip through this section in 1945. Mac and Vic were using an old map which indicated that the John Muir Trail continued down the Middle Fork of the Kings River and over Cartridge Pass. That *was* the official John Muir Trail, until 1939. Rather than follow Mac's route, I chose to continue on the official John Muir Trail and take the easier route over Mather Pass. This was a difficult decision, since Mac described the lower Middle Fork of the Kings River as "one of the happiest bits of water I ever fished over." Besides, I was not entirely sure that the trail over

Cartridge Pass was maintained or still existed.

Stopping to fish a pool on Palisade Creek, just 150 yards from its confluence with the Middle Fork of the Kings River, I saw my first marten. Out of the corner of my eye, I saw what looked like a large squirrel run across the top of a log. As I turned to get a better look at it, he ducked behind a large rock. The rock was only fifteen feet away from me, so a moment later, I watched as he poked his head up from behind it, as if to get a better look at me. I think we were both equally intrigued with one another. After a couple of minutes of staring at me, he grew uninterested, and off he went. What an experience. All the years backpacking and hiking in the Sierra and I had never seen a marten until that day.

A fire had hit most of Palisade Creek Canyon. My guess was that it was eight to twelve years ago. I based this estimate on the growth of the young pine saplings that had sprung up throughout the burn area. The regrowth of other vegetation (especially the aspen trees) indicated this as well. The lodgepole and Jeffery pines were also very healthy. I later learned that it was the Palisade Fire that burned in 2002. It was caused by lightning, considered a managed wildfire, and burned about 1,000 acres.

Halfway up Palisade Creek Canyon, I met a guy from Sacramento that had just given up on completing the John Muir Trail through-hike, north to south. He was visibly disappointed and felt like he had failed. He knew that he would run out of food before finishing the hike at Whitney Portal. I offered some of my food and a few words of encouragement. He declined the food, but accepted the words. I told him that from my perspective, it is all about being here in this part of the Sierra and enjoying every moment. Most people do it in multiple stages, I told him. I suggested that he not focus too much on doing a through-hike, and enjoy the walk in the woods. Come back next year and finish the hike, I suggested. He felt better, turned around, and headed for Bishop Pass. This would take him back down Palisade Creek Canyon and up the Middle Fork of the Kings River to the Dusy Basin Junction at Little Pete Meadow. He was planning on getting to Bishop and taking a bus to Reno, where his wife could pick him up.

At the headwaters of Palisade Creek lies Deer Meadow. I sat on a grassy knoll next to the creek to eat my lunch. My mind seemed to wander for a short while, thinking about how some of these places got their names. As I entered Deer Meadow, I kicked up a doe and two yearlings, and I was staring at Cascade Creek as it truly cascaded down the granite slope from Amphitheater Lake. Yet I'd seen no grouse in Grouse Meadow earlier that morning. Cascade Creek looked so inviting, and I wondered what kind of fish were up in that basin.

The stretch of trail leading to Palisade Lakes from Deer Meadow is called the Golden Staircase. Once it leaves Deer Meadow, it is a steady climb up hundreds of switchbacks and thousands of feet. This was the last section of the John Muir Trail to be built, completed in 1939 by the Civilian Conservation Corps. It is by far the most impressive and difficult section of trail built to this point. I stopped to take a breath and see the view halfway up, noticing that a bright silver dome was following me. It turned out to be a hiker with a silver umbrella attached to his pack to shield him from the sun. It was just so out of place and made me chuckle.

The Palisade Lakes lay in a short valley and are surrounded by a granite fortress. The lakes are teeming with trout to twelve inches, all hybrids of golden and rainbow trout. They hit hard on just about any dry fly. They were anything but finicky. I camped within a clump of boulders and stunted trees next to the outlet of the upper lake. Between the two lakes seemed to be the only place with an adequate campsite. A cold wind was beginning to blow, so I hunkered down behind a big boulder next to a small pine tree and lit my stove to cook dinner.

* * *

The night was windy at the lakes, and I woke to frost on my sleeping bag that morning, an indication that fall had arrived. I packed up quickly and hit the trail as soon as I could. The climb to Mather Pass was steep. Never having been here before, I kept guessing where the pass would be. The scale on the map was too big to be of any real help. That was a game that I had played before. Around most curves in the trail, I would glance at the ridgeline and take a guess at where the trail crested the ridge at the pass. Usually I would try to assess the topography, discounting slopes that were too steep or notches in the ridge that were too ominous. It seemed to keep my mind off the steep slope and step after step of elevation gain.

Alas, I made it. And the wind was still blowing.

I sat on top of the pass with two guys going south to north on the John Muir Trail. For one hiker, this was his sixth full John Muir Trail through-hike. It was his friend's first, and he was having foot issues. He was wearing running shoes and was contemplating cutting the toe out of them. They asked my opinion, which I gave freely. My opinion, I told him, was to wear hiking boots next time, not running shoes. I got a laugh out of them, and we talked about the pros and cons of running shoes versus hiking boots. They were ultra-light guys and felt the pros outweighed the cons. I still disagree. Hiking boots are sturdier, more appropriate, and the best for your feet while hiking the unforgiving terrain of the Sierra.

The view to the south was fantastic. The Upper Basin is dotted with small lakelets and one large unnamed lake at 11,588 feet of elevation. I headed straight for it, cross country, once the switchbacks ended and I was off the ridge.

It was windy there, too. I cast multiple dry flies and several wet leech patterns, to no avail. I kept working one side of the lake and changing flies. I did get one strike from a big fish that came up from the depths for one hit. Maybe he was all alone in this big lake!

I stopped for lunch along South Fork of the Kings River.

While I ate, I laid my sleeping bag on a rock to dry, washed a pair of socks, and soaked my feet in the cold water of the river. This section of river was full of small goldens in the pools. I didn't catch anything over seven inches while using only dry flies.

To get part of the way up the next hurdle, Pinchot Pass, I opted to head for Bench Lake. Mac and Vic attempted to camp at Bench Lake, but got lost due to faint trails coming down from Cartridge Pass. He was told it contained large rainbow, golden, and possibly Eastern brook trout.

When I arrived at Bench Lake, I found that I was all alone, not a single person in sight. I found a great campsite protected from the wind between one of the "fingers" on the eastern side of the lake. Eager to get to studying this striking lake, I explored the east end of the lake and had nothing for the first thirty minutes. I didn't even see a fish. As I worked my way around a point and down one of the fingers, I found a calm spot sheltered from the wind. With poor backcasting clearance, I was only able to get my grasshopper fly out about twenty feet from the boulder where I stood. The water exploded as a thirteen-inch brookie nearly jumped out of the water to snatch my fly. This fish gave me a good fight, and I gave him as much line as he wanted as I brought him to the rocks. He was skinny and had a big head and black spots all over his body and a few red dots near the tail and on the top of the dorsal fin. For a while, I questioned the species of this fish. Was it an Eastern brook trout, a brown trout, or some kind of hybrid? The markings were different and didn't seem to look entirely like any fish I had found in the Sierra before.

I continued along the shoreline and landed six more of these streamlined and powerful athletes between twelve and fifteen inches, plus one twelve-inch rainbow. I must have also had two dozen explosive strikes at my fly without hooking up. The bigger fish seemed to hang out in the shallower fingers of the lake and not in the deep sections facing the center.

Mac and Vic passed up this lake when they began running low on food and time. I wondered what the lake was like in 1945. If it was this good now, it must have been fantastic back then, obviously having received little fishing pressure over the last seventy years.

The Bench Lake Ranger Station was the sight of the search and rescue command post in 1996 that was established to look for missing National Park Service Ranger Randy Morgenson. He was arguably one of the most dedicated and respected rangers in the service. During his twenty-eighth season, he failed to answer his radio during a weekly radio check.

Pair of big brown trout from Bench Lake

Morgenson was having personal problems and began to doubt where he fit into the world around him. These mountains were his home and his lifeblood, and while his life around him was unraveling, he was showing signs of uncertainty. His colleagues mounted an all-out assault on his district to find him. Eric Blehm, author of the book *The Last Season*, tells a fascinating and gripping story about the search and its participants.

Randy's body was eventually found several years later on a seldom-used route. The searchers had previously searched the area and found nothing. It was thought that he was patrolling his district when he fell and was mortally injured. It was a shock and a huge blow to the backcountry rangers working the national parks.

Interestingly, Dad told me a story of an encounter he had with a backcountry ranger in Evolution Valley in 1972. While hiking through a meadow, Dad stopped to pick an unknown wildflower. His intention was to attempt to identify it later when he got to camp. Along the way, he ran into a ranger. Dad pulled out the flower and asked the ranger if he could identify it for him. Angry that someone would actually pick a wildflower, he gave Dad a piece of his mind and began to scold him for picking the wildflowers. After reading the book, Dad thinks it was Randy that he ran into on that trip. Randy was a tireless advocate of the meadows and their plants in the Sierra. He felt that the horse packers, their stock, and hikers were decimating the meadows of the High Sierra.

CHAPTER 7

Bench Lake to Road's End

The morning air was as still as ever—neither a breath of wind nor a ripple on the water. Once the sun began to shine on the water, the bugs and fish became more active. I set off with the same hopper that I was so successful with the night before to see if the morning fishing was better than it had been. To my disappointment, I had only a few hard strikes and a couple of sloppy, weak attempts to grab my fly.

Bench Lake sits a couple miles off the John Muir Trail, something that might account for the lack of visitors. On the way back to the main trail, I stopped and fished the pond near the outlet of the lake. It was full of ten-inch rainbows that were all eager to taste my hopper.

Lake Marjorie was full of active, feisty ten-inch brookies. These were true brookies. Now that I could compare the Bench Lake fish with the Lake Marjorie fish, it was clear that the fish in Bench Lake were in fact brown trout.

I made it to Pinchot Pass and sat atop it with two thoughts. Okay, *three* thoughts. My first thought was that it was a tough climb. One step in front of the other, I constantly sifted through the thousands of thoughts floating through my head on the way to the pass. This particular one came to mind: one of the greatest benefits of getting old and backpacking is that it forces you to frequently stop and look at the scenery.

The second thing that I could not get off of my mind was

that two days prior, a pair of big horn sheep were spotted just under the pass. The two guys that I talked to at the top of Mather Pass saw the sheep. They described it as a *National Geographic* moment as the two sheep stopped about one hundred feet from them just to take a long look at the hikers. Then they turned and walked away as if nothing had happened.

This is such rugged and inhospitable country from our perspective, yet these animals thrive here, and love it. Nicholas had asked me during the section of the trail that we hiked together if big horn sheep could be found in the Sierra. I had originally thought that it was doubtful. But apparently, yes, big horn sheep do live in the Sierra.

The third thought that occupied my mind was that this pass was named after Gifford Pinchot, the first chief of the Forest Service and thought by many to be the father of modern American forestry and forest conservation. He had a big influence on the establishment of our national forests, wilderness areas, and public lands during his long career in public service. Thank you, Mr. Pinchot, for your contributions.

* * *

I hiked the 4,000-foot drop in elevation in seven and a half miles to the confluence of Woods Creek and the South Fork of Woods Creek. My feet, ankles, and knees felt every inch of that hike.

Here is where I needed to deviate from Mac's route once again. I had shipped a food drop to the Cedar Grove Ranger Station (via United States Postal Service). This would be a fifteen-mile hike out to Road's End, where I would need to secure a ride (hitchhike most likely) to Cedar Grove, six miles away.

I walked about three miles down the trail toward Road's End from the Woods Creek junction when I realized that my senses were still attuned to the smells and signs of a recent forest fire. I would get faint and brief whiffs of those familiar smells of a nearby wildfire. Then, I could see a very faint blue haze hanging low in the air down canyon. This was a familiar feeling for me, and I began to get excited.

Sure enough, there was a significant wildfire in the area. With fire operations complete, there were still a few "smokes" across the canyon as the trail meandered through the burn. Flagging was left behind to mark a division separation where a fire line was constructed from the trail to a point uphill on the eastern section of the fire area. The firefighters used water, too. Perhaps they used a portable pump to get water from the creek to the fire. The fire started July 15th and was actively suppressed for a while. It was by then considered a managed wildfire and was posted as such along the trail. It started as a result of a lightning strike on a tree and burned a total of 350 acres.

As I hiked through the burn area, the familiarity and excitement was overwhelming. I spent the last thirty two years of my life in a career as a firefighter, and had just retired months prior. I was trained and qualified in many wildland fire management positions. Many of the wildfires that I had been deployed to over the years suddenly started to come to mind. The assignments, the long, hard days of work, the fun and the joy I had in doing it all was so vivid. I miss that part of my working years.

With the fire behind me and my mind still focused on fire-related thoughts, I was quickly reminded that I was in bear country. I rounded a corner on the trail next to a large Jeffery pine tree when I came upon and startled a solitary male bear (about 150 pounds) as he tore apart a log. He was unaware of my presence and couldn't smell me because I was upwind when I approached him. He stopped when he saw me, hopped up onto the log, and walked off, all while keeping a keen eye on me. After continuing on my hike, I noticed there were bear tracks on the trail, too. Fortunately, they were headed up the canyon.

So many nights on this trip had been above 10,000 feet, where fires are prohibited. A good campsite next to the creek with a perfect fire ring was the ticket. A big fallen pine tree supplied all the firewood that I needed for a raging fire. Knowing that bears were around, I thought briefly about hanging what food I had left, then realized that if a bear wanted the few crumbs left in my food sack, he could have them. I would be out of the wilderness the next day and, frankly, I was too tired to deal with the hassle. I put the last of my food in my OPSAK (Odor Proof Sack) and went to bed after stoking the fire with a few big logs to get the most burn time from my campfire.

With the sun behind the mountains and the darkness fast approaching, I retired to the comfort of my sleeping bag. There was a slight down-canyon breeze that brought faint wafts of wildfire smoke. The familiar sounds of the quaking aspen leaves rustling in the air and the sounds of the water pouring over and around the rocks in the creek were soothing to my weary body. Lying there watching the flames flicker, I made a mental list of some of my favorite trees in the Sierra:

1. Quaking aspen – for the sound they make in the breeze
2. Mountain hemlock – for the conical shape and droopy top
3. Juniper – for their sturdy trunk and ability to grow in a solid rock
4. Ponderosa / Jeffery pine – for their stateliness and bark that smells like vanilla and pineapple
5. *Sequoiadendron giganteum* – do I need to say why?

My ankle was a bit sore in the morning. It felt like I'd pulled a muscle on the inside of my foot, just above the anklebone. The cold water in the creek worked well as I sat on a rock and soaked my foot. Since I didn't have a map for this section of trail, I was not quite sure how far I had to go to get to Road's End. My guess was that it was about twelve miles.

At Upper Paradise Valley (maybe two miles down the trail from where I camped the night before), I came to the bridge that crossed the creek. Oddly, there was a guy sleeping *on* the narrow footbridge. As I climbed up onto the bridge, I woke him. Obviously noticing the perplexed expression on my face, he explained that he was sleeping on the bridge to get away from the ants and bugs on the ground. He reminded me of the typical Santa Cruz bum, with long, dreadlocked hair and dirty, ragged clothes. He quickly jumped up, gathered his sleeping bag, and climbed down off the bridge so I could pass.

I stopped at several of the pools in the valley and fished awhile just to get an understanding of the species of trout that called this section of Woods Creek their home. The creek was full of hungry fish to eight inches. Most were golden, with a few rainbow hybrids.

The entire trek down the canyon was a wonderful and beautiful sight. The valley walls and cliffs are sheer and grand. The creek flows from pool to pool, making it a fine fishing experience, certainly worthy of more exploration. Most sections are difficult to access, leaving only the determined angler the pleasure of its offerings. Someday I would love to spend a week working my way along the entirety of this beauty.

Looking down Woods Creek toward Road's End

During the hike down from the fire area into the ranger's station at Road's End, I was seriously irritated by swarms of "face flies," some kind of gnat that is apparently typical this time of year. They don't bite, sting, or harm you in any way, just irritate the snot out of you. They remind me of World War II Japanese Zero airplanes. They fly around, then out of the blue one will dive bomb, *kamikaze* style, into your eyes, mouth, nose, or ears.

I passed many hikers that employed a variety of methods to keep them at bay. Some would use a head net, something that would keep them off their face and seemed to give good protection from the irritants. I saw a few hikers use a branch of a fir tree tucked under the front of a hat and draped in front of their face. For some reason the flies did not want to fly between the branch and their face. Other hikers employed a bouquet of fern branches and used it as a swatter. The only problem with that, I saw, was the need to continually whisk the ferns in front of their face. The last technique I saw was the hat swatter method. This simple technique uses one's hat to constantly swat the flies in front of your face. Since the DEET insect repellent did not work and I didn't have a net, my hat was the handiest tool to keep the bugs off my face.

Face fly deterrent while hiking Woods Creek

There was really no way around the face flies. I was not looking forward to hiking back up that trail the next day. What I was looking forward to was getting back to the high country and away from the face flies, yellow jackets, and mosquitoes, all of which had been seriously annoying in that area of the Sierra.

* * *

When I arrived at the ranger station at Road's End, I had the pleasure of receiving a "courtesy ride" to Cedar Grove from Russell, the park police officer, a six-mile journey that I was not in the mood to attempt via hitchhiking. At Cedar Grove, all of the hotel rooms were booked, so I was forced to camp at the Sentinel Campground. I was one of three campers in the entire campground, making for a quiet afternoon. I set about to do a little housekeeping and washing clothes. I unpacked and repacked with my next two-week supply of food and took a quick shower. Fording the river to get from the campground to the village was my only option, since the bridge was under construction. That was a tricky feat after dinner and half a bottle of wine! That's right, wine! Along with my food, I had shipped a good bottle of red wine to enjoy when I got to Road's End.

The one piece of technology that I decided to bring along on my trip was a SPOT. It is a personal locator GPS unit that will send up to three personal messages (to up to ten destinations, either cell phone texts or emails) and an emergency SOS signal (the company that makes the SPOT will send the nearest search and rescue team to your location within hours of pushing the button). When I left on this trip, I decided that a nightly check-in with the SPOT would be a good way for everyone to know that I was well. They could also track my progress on Google Maps using the coordinates SPOT transmits to my designated recipients. I had also arranged with Heidi that two days prior to coming out of the backcountry, I would push the button to let her know I was on my way out. (After the trip, I learned that the SPOT only worked about sixty-six percent of the time. I was diligent every night to be sure to send a message and confirm delivery of each message. I guess technology isn't always perfect.)

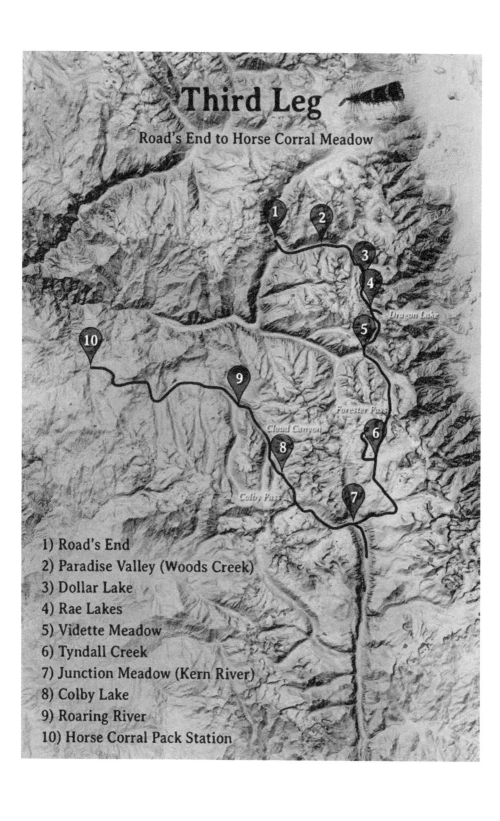

Third Leg

Road's End to Horse Corral Meadow

1) Road's End
2) Paradise Valley (Woods Creek)
3) Dollar Lake
4) Rae Lakes
5) Vidette Meadow
6) Tyndall Creek
7) Junction Meadow (Kern River)
8) Colby Lake
9) Roaring River
10) Horse Corral Pack Station

CHAPTER 8

Road's End to Rae Lakes

The Advantages of Backpacking Solo

- *I can go at my own pace.*
- *I can stop and fish or explore an off trail area without objection.*
- *I can make the decisions. If it is the wrong decision, it only affects me.*
- *I can talk to the squirrels and myself without anyone thinking I am crazy.*
- *I can fart, belch, and expectorate without annoying anyone.*
- *I can stay as dirty and smelly as long as I want without bothering anyone but myself.*

The Disadvantages of Backpacking Solo

- *I miss my wife and family, especially around a fire at night.*
- *I have to carry everything.*
- *I don't have the experience or wisdom of someone else to help me when needed.*

I was on the trail at 8:15 the next morning with a *full* pack. I had almost 3,000 feet of elevation to climb to get back to the John Muir Trail. My goal was to get to Upper Paradise Valley to camp, and with bears in the area, I thought it might be a good idea to use the bear boxes provided. The National Park Service has spent a lot of time and money to install the food lockers in the backcountry in areas where bears and people co-mingle.

Once again I was in my own head, trudging along, thinking about something that I can't even remember now, when I heard a noise and then a hissing sound. I stopped to look back over my shoulder because the sound seemed to come from my pack. Then I realized what the noise was. Stretched out next to the trail not more than three feet from my boots was a rattlesnake. In my presence, he coiled and backed up next to a rock. He must have been about four feet long with nearly eight buttons on his rattle. I was able to get a picture of him before I let him be.

Rattlesnake on trail near Woods Creek

The "face flies" were worse than the day before. I opted, again, to use the fir-branch-under-my-hat method to keep them at bay. This method seemed to work fine—the flies didn't get between the vegetation and my face, and my vision was not too impaired.

It was a slow haul back to the John Muir Trail, seven and a half miles with a full pack. My ankle was sore. I had told Heidi that I would give my ankle a couple of days, and if it was too sore to continue, I would let her know with the SPOT. I sent the message saying that everything was okay and hoped that it went through to her.

The Woods Creek Fire and the Castle Domes

While gathering firewood near camp later that day, two guys crossed the bridge next to the trail. They were heading down to Road's End. Each had just a simple daypack. When I asked where they came from (thinking they were just day hikers coming from their base camp), their reply was that they came from Road's End. I must have had a stupid look on my face because one of them quickly chirped up with an explanation. They were doing the Rae Lakes Loop in one day. Running when they could, they were finishing the forty-two mile loop that took them up and over Glen Pass at 12,000 feet. They had started in the morning when it was still dark and had hoped to finish before dusk. One guy was struggling a bit, but still looked strong. Quite a feat!

The hike up to the John Muir Trail is about five miles from Paradise Valley, all uphill. My ankle felt good and strong, and I was more and more confident that whatever was tweaked in my ankle was quickly un-tweaking. It is hard to get used to a heavy pack while ascending over 3,000 feet in elevation.

The "swinging bridge" at the Woods Creek crossing is one of the most interesting bridges that I have seen in the Sierra. Why was this design used for this bridge? Does the span length have something to do with it? Maybe it was more cost effective to use this style?

The author on the Woods Creek Bridge

I arrived at the creek that drained from Lake 10296 early in the afternoon. Giving my back a break, I dropped my pack at a campsite next to the trail, and after throwing some food and warm clothes in my shoulder sack (I made a simple nylon sack before I left that was just for this purpose), off I went. The 1,300-foot cross-country climb to the lake required using my hands at times to get up and over some of the rock outcroppings.

I followed several game trails up the loose rocky slopes. A doe and her two fawns had gathered in a grassy area on a bench three quarters of the way to the lake. All three bolted when they saw me.

Lake 10296

When I got to the lake, I again concluded that Mom and Dad were more awesome than I had ever realized. To take three boys, ages five, eight, and nine, with backpacks up this cross-country route in 1966 was quite an accomplishment. What were they thinking? Why this lake?

For my brothers and I, this lake seemed to be a symbol of excellent High Sierra trout fishing. It has always been a memory that has never faded and will forever provide me with a benchmark for what fishing was like back then: fantastic! It was some of the best fishing we had ever experienced—big fish, and lots of them, too.

Dad remembers our visit to this little hideaway and recalls that it was just before we had entered the Rae Lakes Basin. It was late in the afternoon and they were concerned we wouldn't reach a lake or good water before dark, so they decided to go cross country to the small lake off to the right of the trail. It didn't look like it was very far or too steep, but it turned out to be a real scramble up a very steep but uniform slope. About halfway up, Mom tripped and stumbled over a yellow jacket nest and in the process got stung several times. By the time we got to the top, it had started raining lightly, with faint thunderclaps all around us. The lake was dimpled with large raindrops. We couldn't tell if fish were rising or not. After making a hasty camp for Mom, who was a little sick from the wasp stings and exertion, we all hit the lake with dry flies and caught a fish on almost every cast. They were all big brookies. We then ate the fish for dinner under the tarp, had a good night's sleep, and then went cross country again to some other group of lakes the next morning. Finally, we dropped back down into the Rae Lakes Basin, which was a *disaster*. Because it was one of the portals from the east slope, the area was trampled, there were piles of crap behind every bush, and the lakes were almost barren of fish, only a few scrawny trout left.

Lake 10296 is an unnamed lake. On the 1958 topographic map, the lake is noted with its elevation: 10,296 feet above sea level. Since it had no name, we all just called it "Lake Ten Two Nine Six." The elevation for this lake has since been updated to 10,315. To me, however, it will always be Lake

10296. It's now *loaded* with brook trout between eight and ten inches, skinny and hungry. I never saw a smaller or larger fish. In the three hours I spent there, I either hooked into or got a strike on just about every cast. I started with a hopper, moved to a yellow-bodied and brown-hackled dry fly (which was shredded by the fish as they attacked it feverishly), then switched to three colors of leech patterns: rust, black, and green. It didn't matter what I threw at them. They were ravenous.

It was interesting how the fish would work themselves into a frenzy over my flies. Frequently, I would have five or six frantic fish all darting after the fly. When one would get hooked, there was usually another darting about and trying to take the fly away from the hooked fish.

What a treat it is to be back at this haven of alpine beauty nestled amongst the granite backdrop. It most definitely sees very little fishing pressure, yet the mystery still remains: why only one size of fish? I suspect that since the fish stocking programs in the park ceased almost two decades ago, the fish population rose to a self-sustaining level, and then tapered off. With a finite food supply, the fish are unable to grow larger due to a sharp increase in competition. Thus, you are left with a fish population of a single size class.

Back at my pack, I had a decision to make. Do I set up camp here or push on to Dollar Lake for the night? It was 5:30 and I felt I had enough energy to make the gentle climb to Dollar Lake, so off I went. It was a little farther than I had anticipated, and I arrived with just enough light to make camp, take a quick rinse in the lake, eat dinner, and go to bed.

A cool down-canyon breeze greeted me as I awoke the next morning. It made getting out of my warm sleeping bag that much harder. If it weren't for a full bladder that was screaming for relief, I wouldn't have gotten out of bed until noon.

Once the breeze died down and the sun began to shine, I started to notice a few small ripples on the water—the work of the resident brookies. I had a yellow Stimulator on my leader, so

I cast a few places just to see what species of trout they might be. They were all small, and took my fly actively in the still morning water.

Camp at Dollar Lake

* * *

I slid my pack off when I arrived at the shore of the first of the Rae Lakes and cast a big lime-green Humpy into the water. In just a few short casts I had landed two, hooked into and lost three, and had a dozen strikes. They all seemed to exhibit the same "brookie behavior" of Lake 10296—frenzied and seemingly ravenous. It brought a smile to my face, and I enjoyed the interaction very much. The sun was shining and the air was warm, a wonderful combination that made me want to stay longer.

In 1945, Mac found the fishing to be disappointing, with

large fifteen-inch brook and rainbow trout with emaciated bodies and huge heads. Of his experience, he wrote that there were too many fish and food was too scant. Even back then, this area was full of people and noise. When he arrived, someone had hauled in (on mule back) a portable boat with an outboard motor and had completely nullified the surrounding beauty.

I settled into a campsite near the Upper and Middle Rae Lakes. Since it was a very popular place that was usually full of people and bears, the site had a food storage locker. Hiking the John Muir Trail, a father and his adult son, John and Towner Menefee, from Bend, Oregon, were camped next to me. John came in yesterday over Kearsarge and Glen Passes with a seventy-pound pack to resupply his son's pack for the last section of the trip. John planned to join his son on the last leg of the trek.

Lower Rae Lake

It was still early and I was itching to make the climb to

Dragon Lake. Mac wrote tales of huge trout (lunkers to three feet) that would not take a fly. He pulled out big fish that were, as he called them, "steelheads." Attempting to land a three-foot trout proved too much for Mac, and he said that "no one could ever land a dragon." He fished with a #10 Cutthroat, a black gnat, and a #4 Bucktail Carson steelhead fly. I yearned to slay a dragon of my own. All along this trek, I had secretly dreamed of landing a huge lunker, just to prove that big fish can still survive in these high-reaching waters.

Scott remembers our family detour to Dragon Lake while camped at the Rae Lakes in 1966. The following is his account:

We had heard the stories about Dragon Lake and it's legendary large steelhead-looking trout, so we all took a day-hike detour to check it out for ourselves. It was an overcast day, the sky a silvery-gray, the water was a deep, dark gray color and was surrounded by granite-gray mountains. We had to go back down to our base camp so we couldn't wait for the evening glass-off and the prime fishing that always seems to happen when the wind dies down. We all were unsuccessful after several hours, and after the incredible successes of Lake 10296 days before, us kids all got bored easily. Meanwhile, our mother persevered. As us kids were playing alongside the lake, a "whoop" from down the shore made us all look up to see Mom with her fly rod doubled over. We rushed to her as she battled the largest trout any of us had ever seen! She had to work it over to a sandy beach so she could carefully drag the enormous silver "dragon" up onto the shore. Once up on the sand, it flipped off of the fly and Eric and I immediately dove on it to keep it from flopping back into the water. The rumor was true! We have no record of how big it actually was, but we guessed it to be about eighteen inches and fat, far bigger than anything we had ever seen before in our High

Sierra trips. I just remember being so impressed that my mother could catch a fish that huge—bigger than our dad could catch!

From my camp, I could see the Dragon Lake outlet creek as it tumbled down the granite rocks toward Upper Rae Lake. I started up the hill through the rocks, cross country, intending to follow the creek as much as possible. The map showed that there was no trail to the lake. I didn't get very far when I ran into a trail. It was faint, not maintained or well traveled, and not well marked, either. A few ducks were placed along the way to mark the route. But a trail is a trail, and it lead me to Dragon Lake.

There were no "lunkers to three feet." There were no "steelheads." There were, however, a lot of eight to twelve-inch brookies that freely attacked and grabbed just about anything I threw at them. What a fun time. Dragon Lake is beautiful and deserves to have a reputation of growing and harboring big trout.

Fishing Dragon Lake

I used my assortment of wet leech fly patterns with different colors, a grasshopper, and a lime-green Humpy to catch the bulk of my fish. Just for fun, I threw on a spinning lure that I found along the shore next to a big rock. Even with the shank of the hook broken and the point and barb missing, I landed three fish. Like the lower Rae Lake, I did not want to leave this little bit of paradise. The solitude, warm sunshine, plenty of fish to keep any angler company, and spectacular views of the surrounding mountains made for a near perfect experience. Standing on the shore and looking at the mountain range surrounding the lake, I could not see the "dragon" formed in the rocks that gave this lake its name.

Baby dragon - brookie from Dragon Lake

Mac with steelhead from Dragon Lake, circa 1945

* * *

Many fly fishing anglers believe that they belong to an elite group of individuals, whether the angler views himself an amateur entomologist, an ichthyologist, a hydrologist, or an expert with fly tackle. I have always considered myself more or less self-taught, having only been coached by my parents as a kid. I love fly fishing and am constantly attempting to hone my skills and knowledge of the sport. Mac, however, has been recognized many times as an expert High Sierra fly fishing angler, and specifically, an expert on fly fishing for golden trout. When I set out on this endeavor, I wanted to compare the more than six decades of change in the Sierra fisheries, fly fishing tackle, and these granite-laden mountains.

In his book, Mac talks a lot about his fishing gear and the techniques that he used. Even though he appears to be solely fly fishing, he noted that when he went over Donohue Pass he discarded gear that he thought was too heavy and did not need, like a jar of salmon eggs and a half pound of lead weights. What would a fly fisherman do with salmon eggs and a half-pound of lead? He did come to conclude that he would take fish on a fly, or no fish at all.

Mac carried a seven-foot fly rod, but there was no mention of its make and model. In 1945, the fly rod of choice was most likely one of bamboo construction. Of the few pictures in his book that depict a rod and reel, it is hard to tell if the rod is bamboo or not. I chose to bring two fly rods. One is an old two-piece graphite rod (model GRF 1000) made by Courtland. It is a nine-foot, five/six weight rod that I bought at a garage sale for a few bucks. So, it is not a rod of great quality, but it is a rod of great purpose. The second rod is a two-piece, seven-foot rod that Keith Mellor and Bill Ekwall (my old crew at the fire station, until they retired) gave to me as a retirement gift. It is a three weight from Cabela's. I love this rod. It is great for the small creeks and streams. The nine-foot rod, I found, was ideal for the lakes, as I could cast much farther with its sturdier and longer profile.

Mac's reel of choice was not mentioned in his books. As with his rod, I am not able to discern his reel's make or model from the photographs in his book. I only brought one reel, and that was the reel that came with the rod Keith and Bill gave me. It is also from Cabelas and has a good drag that is perfect for this type of fishing in the Sierra, whether on a river or a lake.

Mac often mentions the need to soak his leaders. He used leaders made from cat gut that needed to soak to become soft; otherwise they would be too brittle and break. He suggested, at the end of his book, a tapered leader made by Hardy Brothers that sells for "six bits." How much is six bits, you might ask? Well, six bits converts to seventy-five cents, as a "bit" is equal to twelve and a half cents. I only fly fish with tapered monofilament leaders. They are easy and relatively inexpensive.

We can talk a lot about the flies that Mac used in the High

Sierra. He seemed to be very clear and particular about his talk of certain flies, hook size, etc. The flies that were popular in 1945 are basically ancient history for today's fly angler. However, Mac always referred to them as if the angler reader would understand what they were and how they were commonly fished. Below is a list of some of the flies Mac used:

- Silver Doctor
- Coachman
- Black gnat
- Gray Hackle, yellow body
- Rio Grande King
- McGinty
- Gray Hackle, peacock body
- Captain
- Mosquito
- Cutthroat – white wing, red body, and black hackle (this was Mac's "pet Sierra fly")
- #4BucktailCarson

The fishing techniques Mac typically used included targeting fish that he could see, commonly called "sight fishing." I can only imagine that in 1945, with little fishing pressure and many larger fish, this was a technique that worked very well. In this day and age, with the significant changes in the fisheries of the High Sierra, I have found that sight fishing is only an occasional option. I have employed it, usually in lakes, on the small "cruiser" fish as they swim close to shore looking for food. Typically, the technique most commonly used would be that of "blind casting," and hoping that a fish will see the fly land on the water and go after it.

On one occasion, Mac talked about using two flies. One is "dropped" below the first using a "snelled" fly. The idea is simple: a dry fly is drifted on the surface of the water with a small nymph fly tied to the bend of the dry fly hook. It is thus suspended under the water, increasing your odds of catching a fish. Mac did manage to hook and land two fish at once. I use this method often, usually on the larger rivers and streams where there is ample room to backcast and plenty of depth so that the dropped fly won't get hung up on the bottom or on submerged debris.

I also use a silicone fly floatant that is applied periodically to the fly, giving it a better floating ability. As a kid, I was taught to bring the fly up off the water and false cast several times before bringing the fly back onto the water. This allowed the fly to "dry" and shed the small water droplets to retain its natural floating abilities. Mac had to rely on this technique, too.

CHAPTER 9

Rae Lake to Tyndall Creek

Glen Pass was next. As I passed John and Towner's camp, they roused enough to inquire about camping together again at Vidette Meadow. That way, we could have a fire and cook a delicious fish dinner. They wanted to fish Dragon Lake and bring enough fish for all of us to eat. Quick plans were made, and off I went. The trail to the pass was, like so many before, a trail building marvel. A California Conservation Corps crew was busy getting tools and gear together to start the day's work of rebuilding the trail just under the pass. I made sure to thank them, mostly young men and a few women, for their work. I also commented on what a great job they were doing. I could tell my comments were greatly appreciated.

My initial thought was to stop at Bullfrog Lake to fish, but when I passed two groups of day hikers on their way to fish Charlot Lake, both groups suggested that I not waste my time there. I skipped Bullfrog Lake. In 1945, this lake was said to contain big Loch Leven trout to ten pounds. Not these days, apparently!

When I arrived at Vidette Meadow, I found a good campsite about a half mile above the meadow. I left a note next to the trail nailed to a tree with a wooden peg that read "John and Towner – Fish dinner tonight?" and drew an arrow pointing the way. I was setting up camp when a backcountry ranger walked up. His name was Rick Sanger, a pleasant man from

Grass Valley. He jokingly inquired as to whether there would be enough fish for him, too. We had a great visit talking about bears, fish, his job, and fires. He was on patrol, headed up the canyon to an area where hikers usually camp and illegally build campfires.

Unnamed lake looking south from Glen Pass

* * *

I fished Bubbs Creek from the campsite all the way up to the "falls." It was difficult fishing due to the amount of brush along the banks of the creek. When I could get to a pool and not spook its inhabitants, I did well and kept three nine-inch fish for dinner, one brookie and two rainbow hybrids. All three took dry flies (hopper, green Stimulator, and a white-winged, red-bodied Humpy). I figured they would be a fine addition to the Dragon

Lake trout that John and Towner would bring back.

Golden and brown trout taken from Bubbs Creek, Vidette Meadow

When I got back to camp, John and Towner were there. They had already collected enough firewood for the night and had a fire roaring in the fire pit. It had just started to rain—not hard, but enough to get everything damp, and just enough to be annoying.

Towner went off to catch a few fish for dinner since they'd decided not to go to Dragon Lake and had arrived back at camp empty handed. John and I stayed back, tended the fire, and talked while under their umbrellas. Yes, umbrellas. They each had an umbrella and used them not only for rain protection, but for sun protection, too.

We cooked the trout, seasoned with wild onions, wild sage, and the famous "Menefee spice," in foil over the fire. They were the best tasting trout I had had yet. We enjoyed a great evening just hanging by the fire and talking well into the night. They are fine people, and we vowed to keep in contact and to stick together one more night.

The next morning, we set off with the goal to get over Forester Pass (13,200 feet), fish the two lakes below the pass on the south side, and camp near Tyndall Junction.

Looking back into Bubbs Creek and the Kearsarge Pinnacles

We were successful on all three accounts. Forester Pass is the highest pass on the John Muir Trail and the Pacific Crest Trail. Although the three of us set out together, we did not make it to the pass together. They were much faster at the uphill sections than I was. I caught up to them at the second lake below the pass. The two lakes appeared fishless, no sign or sight of any fish. Surprisingly, Mac and his hiking partner, Vic, found the upper lake to contain a few very large fish that they did not land, and the lower lake supported a large population of pure golden trout. The wind and rain arrived again, so we chose to give up on any more exploration of the lakes and kept moving instead.

Looking up to the Kings-Kern Divide and Mt. Stanford

We arrived at Tyndall Junction and found a good campsite next to the creek where the trail to the ranger station splits off from the main trail. I fished Tyndall Creek that evening and had to keep two beautiful goldens at eight and nine inches because they both swallowed the hooks. Most of the fish I caught were goldens; only two fish I landed were brookies.

With our handshakes and farewells completed the following morning, I took off for Lake South America. It was a three-mile hike along a not-too-frequently-used trial. Mac talked about the big goldens that were twenty-four inches long and would not take his flies. He was, however, able to land an eighteen-incher that he accidentally snagged.

Camp at Tyndall Creek

With thoughts of exploring new territory, my strides were bounding. About a mile west of the John Muir Trail is the lakelet where Vic and Mac camped when they passed through here. Still nameless, I veered off the faint trail to try my luck in this small and shallow flake of water. Fishless! Mac and Vic had great success with this lake. They found that not a single fish was less than fifteen inches, and all were brightly colored and magnificent fighters.

When I got back on the trail at the top of the ridge to the west, I could see a bigger lake further west and a smaller lake up the basin and to the right. I chose to continue to Lake South America and fish the bigger lake on the return hike.

Turning around, I looked east from atop a small ridge and had a commanding view of the Upper Tyndall Creek area. The creek is small and meanders through the barren landscape. It looked like it should be in Mongolia or someplace similar. Mac referred to it as a fly fisherman's dream: a creek that is a series of one pool cascading into another, full of nine-inch golden trout, and virtually no brush or trees to foul your backcast.

Back on the trail, I passed a very small lake at the head of the basin, just before the short and steep climb over a small pass to Lake South America. There was a breeze that rippled the water as I approached the shore. My hopes of it containing any fish were very low, considering the small lakelet I had visited just minutes prior.

Just for the hell of it, I figured that I had better at least cast a few flies to confirm there really were no fish. From atop a rock next to the shore, I stripped line off my reel to get ready to cast. Suddenly a fish rose to energetically attack a bug on the water's surface, falling back into the water with a loud splash. My first cast, and almost every cast thereafter, either yielded a strike or landed a fish.

This small lake was full of ten- to twelve-inch brookies. All were eager and excited to attack any fly that I offered. Wet flies (leeches and Woolly Buggers) or dry flies (yellow jacket and hoppers); it did not matter. Other anglers knew about this little gem, too. There were dozens of moldy fish heads and gut remnants in the water next to one big rock in a few feet of water.

The entire forty-five minutes I spent there was pure joy—so much so that I could not get out of my mind how much Heidi would love to fish here. It was easy to cast into, there were lots of fun fish to catch, and it would be just the two of us in such a remote place. I named the lake "Lake Heidi" since it did not have a name, and it is a fitting tribute since both are so beautiful.

Lake Heidi

The climb away from Lake Heidi up and over the shallow, narrow "pass" to Lake South America was much steeper than I had thought. A few horses were the last travelers along the faint trail, their hoof prints sunken in the soft, decomposed granitic sand. Hardened by the last few rain storms, the hoof prints provided me with decent footholds from which to step.

In the July 14, 1952 issue of *Life Magazine*, Edward Clark, a photographer, accompanied Mac on a fishing trip into the Kern River area. They packed on horseback out of Mineral King to fish for golden and Gilbert rainbow trout inhabiting the lakes and creeks. One photo in the article in particular stands out to me. It is a picture of two men on horseback and their stock animals descending a rather steep, rocky slope. In the background are two small lakes. The closest lake is identifiably Lake Heidi. A comparison of the pictures that I took and the one in the *Life* article is unmistakable. I happened to climb up the hill, along a seldom-used trail, and be in the very same spot that Mac travelled over sixty years earlier.

A marmot was wandering about near the trail, so I stopped to watch him and to take a few pictures. It was a great opportunity to catch my breath, too. He seemed somewhat interested in me. We stood there, almost frozen, and checked each other out while I was able to slowly creep within ten feet of him.

My attention once again turned to Lake South America, with thoughts of big fish that I hoped would still be there. I arrived to get my first glimpse of this beautiful lake and the deep blue colors that are in stark contrast to the gray-colored granite walls of the cliffs behind it. The wind picked up and continued while I explored its shore. The lake is aptly named, roughly the shape of the continent from which it takes its name.

Lake South America

I fished up the coasts of Argentina, Uruguay, and most of Brazil with no luck; not even a sign of a fish. The coast of Chile was much shallower, so I headed that way to explore. Still nothing, and it was like that all the way through Peru and Ecuador.

Why is this lake also fishless? It certainly could maintain a healthy population of fish. Over thirty years ago, my brother Scott and his wife Lauri backpacked to this very same lake. They, like Mac, also found big fish that would not take a fly. The owner of the Horse Corral Pack Station, Mr. Charley Mills, has subsequently told me that the lake does contain big fish. Another mystery!

Disappointed, I turned my attention to getting back to my pack and setting another course of action. I veered off the trail to prospect the biggest of the unnamed lakes on my return trip to Tyndall Creek. I found that the creek between Lake Heidi and the big lake below it held fish in the bigger pools. This, I thought, was a good sign that there might be fish in the bigger lake. However, it too was fishless. I worked my way around most of the shore with no sign of fish.

On my way back, I was traversing cross country from the big unnamed lake when I startled two deer. Both were antlerless. One was very light gray in color and the other very brown, almost chestnut. The odd thing was that when they spotted me, they both squatted on their hind legs, almost sitting on the ground like a dog, and froze to watch me. I have never seen deer do that, and I still wonder what that behavior signifies.

CHAPTER 10

Tyndall Creek to Junction Meadow

Back at my pack, with my food supply on target now (John and Towner gave me three freeze-dried dinners that they were not going to need) and my stove fuel being *very* low, I reviewed my options. Figuring I had enough fuel for one, possibly two, days, I decided to make a change in my itinerary. Rather than spend the afternoon fishing the Upper Tyndall Creek area and spend the night in the area (where I need to use the stove to cook), I decided to press on to Wallace Creek.

The hike to Wallace Creek was an easy four and a half miles across and through Bighorn Plateau. The best view of Mt. Whitney yet was from the plateau. I took quite a few pictures of this magnificent mountain range.

When I reached the trail junction at Wallace Creek, there were five or six groups already camped at the sites along the creek. At an elevation of 10,400 feet, I would still need to use my stove to cook. So, another decision was made. I would forego the exploration of Wallace Lake and Wales Lake. The lack of stove fuel, low food, and time were all against me.

I headed down the Wallace Creek drainage to the Kern River. I wanted to stop and fish several locations of Wallace Creek, but most of it was quite a distance from the trail and would take too much time to explore properly. I stumbled into a camp along the Kern River with a food storage locker at about seven in the evening. I had enough light to quickly gather firewood, make a fire, set up my sleeping area, eat dinner, brush my teeth, and get to bed. I was still dirty and needed to clean up, but was too tired to do so.

Mt. Whitney from Bighorn Plateau

Waking up leisurely in the outdoors is not something that I have ever been able to do. The sounds of the forest come alive, almost like an alarm clock. The birds are chirping, squirrels are chewing at pine cones and letting them drop, and the sounds of the water in the river won't let me stay asleep too long.

I stole a pine cone from a squirrel (technically a Sierra chickaree). He was working in a tree above me and had chewed off a cone and let it fall to the ground, landing about fifteen feet from my sleeping bag. I had always wanted to try freshly roasted pine nuts. I set it on the fire and roasted it while I had my morning coffee. The heat melted the pitch and opened all the bracts on the cone to reveal two nuts attached to "wings" tucked inside each bract. I popped them out of the wings and into my sierra cup. Most were quite meaty and soft in texture and had a mild pine flavor; however, a few were dry and tasted strongly of pine pitch. Overall, I enjoyed the experience.

Junction Meadow camp

Since I didn't fish Wallace Creek the day before on my way down the canyon, I decided to explore the creek above the High Sierra Trail crossing. It would have been an easy fishing creek if it weren't for the brush. The creek gradually descends along the alluvial slope after leaving the steep canyon from above. The pools are small and full of trout. Most fish were rainbows, specifically the famous Gilbert rainbow that Mac raved about. He described them as having profuse spots over the entire body, with a broad rose-colored band from the gill plate to the anal fin. His description of this beauty was spot on.

Oddly, I also caught several golden and brown trout. The brown trout had the usual red spots with a whitish halo circling each spot, were olive in color on their bellies, and possessed black spots all over. All the Wallace Creek fish were eight to eleven inches long, and took the yellow Stimulator fly freely and often slowly.

I spent the rest of the morning prospecting the Kern River below Junction Meadow. The river slowly twists through a thick forest of mostly lodgepole pine. The forest was severely overgrown and full of downed trees. This made following the river very difficult. I finally resorted to getting out onto the trail and hiking several miles downstream to where access was allowable for easy fishing. This stretch of the Kern River is a slow and shallow ramble with short, confined drops through narrow sets of riffles.

I only caught one eleven-incher out of the river below camp. He took the Copper John nymph that was dropped below a grasshopper. Full of energy, he darted from one side of the pool to the other. Once he tired, I was able to drag him ashore between two rocks on the bank of the river.

After lunch, I fished upstream from camp and into the Upper Kern River Gorge. What a pleasant fishing experience. I basically rock-hopped up the river and fished each pool. In two hours, I must have landed two dozen Gilbert rainbows and had five times that many strikes or self-extricating hook-ups. The fish seemed to favor the Copper John, but also took a lime-green Humpy, black and white Stimulator, and elk hair caddis without too much coaxing.

The campsite I picked was one of four in the Junction Meadow area. Next to my site was a big metal food storage locker, installed by the park service and resting right next to a big pine tree. I noticed a square notch carved in the tree about six inches square, four inches deep, and about four and a half feet off the ground. The notch had obviously been there for a while; the tree's bark had grown over the edges in an attempt to heal itself. Curious, I glanced over my right shoulder and noticed an identical notch in a tree about twelve feet away. A post or board must have once been held up and positioned between these two notches, I thought. Maybe a hitching post for horses? Some sort of camp furniture? I was puzzled. When I returned from my trip and had the opportunity to view the slides from my mom's 1945 trip, one picture stood out. Over the shoulder of a packer smoking trout over a fire is what I believe to be the very same trees with the notches. A table was built between the two trees. What are the odds that I inadvertently camped in the very same site?

First Gilbert rainbow from Upper Kern River

I believe this is also the same site where Mac camped in 1952 when he took the small group from *Life Magazine* on a horse packing trip. One of the photos shows their camp with very similar terrain.

*Packer smoking trout at Camp G.R. Goldman in 1945,
Junction Meadow
(notched tree with table in background)*

Camp G.R. Goldman, Junction Meadow, 1945

I felt honored and grateful to be camped on the Kern River and fishing the same waters. I can see why fishermen, horsemen, backpackers, and outdoor enthusiasts want to be here. The beauty, grandeur, and magic of the Kern River Valley are unmatched in the Sierra.

Full as a tick after three big Gilbert rainbow trout cooked in foil over a fire, complemented with pasta and a cup of soup, I spent the evening contemplating my journey. In reflection, the fishing had been absolutely incredible—way beyond my expectations. I found fish in water where I did not expect to find fish. I fished lakes that should contain trout, only to find them fishless. There were creeks full of small golden trout, and I was amazed to find waters that had not changed, even after over forty years. Many fishermen before me experienced a level of fishing that today's anglers will never see. I feel, however, that my fishing experience over the month that I was on my journey has been one that many of today's anglers don't get, either.

Fishing the falls along the Kern River Gorge

145

I planned to tackle Colby Pass the following day—eight and a half miles and almost a 4,000-foot climb in elevation. It would be the last major hurdle of the trip and the ninth pass. I had already traversed Donohue, Island, Silver, Seldon, Muir, Mather, Pinchot, and Forester Passes. What's one more?

Up to this point, I intended to head down the Kern River to fish, wanting to stop at the Kern River Hot Springs, fish Golden Trout Creek, and possibly see the Old Lewis Camp. Given my low food and fuel situation and the fact that I lacked the proper maps (my maps don't cover the southern Kern River area), I chose to skip these highlights. My goals that I set prior to launching my journey were to fish the waters that Mac fished, retrace his routes as much as possible, and reflect on what changes I was able to note. I felt like I had been successful, and now I could focus on my next set of goals: following the route that my great-grandfather took in 1945 with my mother.

It was at this point on the trip that I finally figured out the name of a particular species of pine growing near the Rae Lakes and on Bighorn Plateau. When I had arrived at the Rae Lakes and met John and Towner, John, out of the blue, asked me if I knew anything about trees. After explaining to him that I had studied dendrology and had a degree in forestry from Humboldt State University, he asked the names of the trees we had camped under at the Rae Lakes. One was a lodgepole, but the other had me completely befuddled. On the mature trees, the bark was deep red in color and had strong, deep fissures. The bark was not scaly like the Jeffery pines. The cones were similar in shape to the Jeffery, only smaller. The trees were bigger and thicker than the lodgepole. Its needles were four per fascicle and were born completely around the twig, much further from the terminus than the lodgepole. The trees grew in pure stands, but also in association with the lodgepole. It seemed to live long, and many that had died were still standing. I hiked through a pure stand of these magnificent trees up on Bighorn Plateau and near Tyndall Creek.

In the food locker at my camp at Junction Meadow, I found a laminated educational flier about that very same tree, presented by the park service. The tree is a foxtail pine, *Pinus balfouriana*. It's a sub-alpine resident only found in the southern Sierra Nevada and the Klamath Mountains of California, and it can live for over 2,000 years. Mystery solved!

Foxtail pine snag, Tyndall Creek area

CHAPTER 11

Junction Meadows to Horse Corral Pack Station

The climb over Colby Pass, 4,000 feet in elevation in eight and a half miles through the Kern-Kaweah area, was a bugger! My legs, back, and body felt ripped to pieces. I scrambled to the top of the pass in the early afternoon while the sun was at its highest and the heat was intense. Glad that it was over, I sat in a notch on the ridge and gazed at Colby Lake below. Seventy years ago, the Goldman party stood on that very spot, joyous that they, too, were in such a beautiful place.

Meadow before reaching Colby Pass

Colby Pass, 1945, with the Goldman group

Colby Pass, 1945, with Edward A., Helen, George R., and Barbara

Colby Pass

During my climb, I kept my mind occupied, thinking about some of the things that I missed: a comfortable chair, a glass of good red wine, chocolate, my bed with clean sheets, a shower with hot water, ice, escalators, and the comfort of a toilet seat. My list is no way categorized by importance. It has been thirty days since I walked away from Tuolumne Meadows. I knew that thirty days after I return home, a similar list would be reflected in my head about those wilderness things that I would be missing.

Once I turned off the John Muir Trail at the Wallace Creek Junction, I only saw ten or so people in a day and a half. Leaving Junction Meadow for Colby Pass was a solitary journey. The route up and over Colby Pass wasn't a major trail, but it was official, and it *was* maintained, just how I like it—just like the old days!

I made easy time getting down the steep slope to Colby Lake. After a quick rest, I rigged up my rod with a yellow Stimulator and off I went to fish the northwest shore of the lake. It appeared to be a bit more attractive and the wind was more favorable for casting.

Along the shore, I could see the typical "cruisers." They seemed to not be too bothered by my presence. Just about every fish that I spotted took the fly as it was presented. *Great odds for catching fish*, I thought. I then moved to where the inlet creek drains into the lake as the sun dipped down behind the mountains. For fifteen minutes, I nearly caught a fish every cast. Only a couple of casts came up empty. All the fish were seven to nine inches and golden or golden hybrid. My guess is that they hybridized with a rainbow, given the bright rose colors on the gill plate, copious spots, and faint shimmer to the sides. All had the telltale parr marks and white-tipped ventral and anal fins of a golden trout.

Colby Lake from camp

151

An evening stroll with a cup of tea was the perfect end to an otherwise tough day. The creek flowing out of Colby Lake was alive with small fish jumping and feeding, but I was too tired to fish. I walked to the outlet creek and peered down into Cloud Canyon. The Whaleback sat directly in front of me, and it was a wonderfully impressive sight. It is a sharp, knife-like ridge of rock that rises 2,000 feet to split the upper reaches of the canyon.

George R. Goldman looking up at Colby Pass

* * *

With no morning fire to warm me or boil water, I used what fuel I had left for the stove to boil water for my morning routine. I was packed and on the trail before the sun's rays reached the lake. It would be at least an hour and a half before they would.

152

Cloud Canyon, 1945

Descending down into the canyon to the east of the Whaleback, the trail was steep. The valley below was the typical, glaciated U-shape, a small creek trickling down its center. Where it joined the outflow creek from Colby Lake, its pools were full of small golden trout, busy going after any fly or bug that landed on the water. The morning air was just starting to warm, which in turn increased the activity of the small insects in the meadow. Where the trail rounded the heel of the Whaleback, the view into Cloud Canyon and down to Big Wet Meadow was magnificent, with the ridges on either side built of slick granite.

As I made my way down into Cloud Canyon to Brewer Creek, I only saw one person. The trail was gentle and easy walking, with signs that it was a popular route for horsemen and their stock.

When I arrived at Brewer Creek, there was a National Park Service Trail Assessment Crew finishing a break. I inquired as to whether or not there was, or ever has been, a trail to Brewer Lake. The crew leader did not think there ever was a trail. However, he said his packer, who has been working the area since the mid-1970s, had talked about getting stock up to the lake before, but he was unsure how the packer did so.

Family pack trip from Horse Corral to Brewer Lakes
Moraine Ridge, Colby Pass, and the Whaleback, August 1967

Once more, I realized that Mom and Dad did it again. In 1967, they took four kids (ages five, seven, ten, and eleven) on a cross-country, uphill trek to camp at another out-of-the-way lake, making the 3,000-foot elevation climb to Big Brewer Lake.

When I arrived at the trail junction at Scaffold Meadows, the local backcountry ranger, Cindy Wood, had just returned to the station with her stock and a work crew. She has been a ranger at the station for the last nine years. I asked her what she knew about a trail to Brewer Lake. She replied that there were actually three. They are not formal trails, but are somewhat marked with ducks. Two trails take off from the trail to Avalanche Pass and follow along Moraine Ridge. She told me that she has taken stock on those routes before. The third takes off from the John Muir Trail near Brewer Creek and follows the south side of the creek. Near the top, the trail switches and follows the north side of the creek to the lake.

If Mom and Dad took a trail, it would most likely have been the third. I say that because on that trip we camped at Grasshopper Camp. It is along the John Muir Trail, just down the canyon from Brewer Creek. It has since been "minimized" to just a fire ring by the National Park Service. In the pictures from our 1967 family trip, the camp was adorned with log furniture to include tables, chairs, and all sorts of camp "upgrades." That most likely would have been the location where they took off up the side of the canyon walls to Brewer Lake.

Grasshopper Camp in Cloud Canyon, 1967

Big Brewer Lake at 11,700 ft. and Mt. Brewer, 1967

Sitting on the bank of Roaring River, I could not stop thinking about some of the family traditions and customs on our backpacking trips. Until recently, I thought everyone backpacked the same way as we did. When we arrived at camp, we all had to pitch in and help set up camp and collect firewood before we could go fishing or explore.

Camp usually consisted of a campfire with a useful cooking area (which sometimes meant searching to find that perfect big flat rock to use as a table). We *always* cooked over a fire. The fire grates we used were made by my uncle, Frank, and I still use them today. We used a cooking kit that consisted of multiple aluminum cook pots that would nest inside one another. For cooking pancakes, powdered eggs, or fish, we always brought a square Teflon frying pan. I still have it and use it on occasional backpack trips, even though it is heavy and over fifty years old.

We all slept together on one tarp, lined up like sardines in a can. Mom had a way of being able to sit under her unzipped sleeping bag and completely and privately change her clothes. When it rained we used Visqueen to act as a rain fly suspended between trees or rocks, although Dad says we once used tube tents on one trip and got soaked. We never used a tent again. The best part about not using a tent was the game we would play when we all climbed into our bags. The idea was to be the first one to spot a shooting star or satellite. In the 1960s, satellites were very few and far between, and we usually fell asleep before seeing one. It's an entirely different story today.

While hiking along a trail, it was the job of the first person in line to yell out the word "downhill" when the trail started its downward trajectory. That way everyone knew to expect, and to look forward to the coming hike. No one liked hiking uphill! If bears were around, we would hang our food in a tree. We never treated our water, and would drink freely right from the stream, river, or lake. Usually, we would hike with our Sierra cups tucked under our belts for easy access.

Bruce family sleeping arrangement, 1970

Breakfast of fish, pancakes, and eggs over a fire, 1968

Mom made a lot of our backpacking equipment, including our sleeping bags, ponchos, wool shirts, and backpacks. Uncle Frank made me and my sister, Tammi, our first backpacks. It was made from a welded aluminum tube and had canvas supports and padded shoulder straps. At one point, Mom made a bag for mine, too. I still have that first pack. My son, Justin, actually used it on his first few trips, carrying only our sleeping bags and sleeping pads lashed to the frame.

Before each trip, Mom would make sure that we all had our own bandana and stick of Chapstick. Weeks before each trip, we would fill the living room floor with everyone's gear. There was always the usual swapping of gear as one sibling outgrew one item and the next in line gained possession of it. A hat was another must-have. Boy Scout fifty-mile hats (each year the hats were a different color or style) were frequently worn and were a kind of badge of honor for us boys.

* * *

I camped next to Roaring River, reduced to a timid meow. I found a site with a fire ring and firewood already stacked for the next visitor. The fire pit even came with a grate! A big roaring fire was a welcome addition. I was tired, nearing the end of my trip, and missing my family; what better way to fend off the lonely feelings! The site was just downstream from the "swinging" gate below Scaffold Meadows. I needed to get as far away from the horses and stock animals in the area. I stayed up as long as I could that night, just to soak it all in. It was my last night in the wilderness.

Roaring River is a great river to fish. The channel is full of rocks and boulders, the water dropping from pool to pool with plentiful pocket water for fish to be found. Fishing that section is easy since there is little brush to foul a backcast. All I have to do is hop from rock to rock to fish each pool. I tend to favor small rivers and creeks. Am I too particular when it comes to this type of angling? I don't think so; it just seems to be where I am more familiar and comfortable.

The fish were spooked easily, and I needed to sneak up on each pool to get my fly on the water without detection. I did notice that once I spooked the fish in a pool, they would not hit my fly. I would be forced to move on to the next pool.

I brought back three fish for dinner. Two were rainbows of about nine inches. The third was a husky eleven-inch brown trout that slammed my fly, and then proceeded to thrash about in the pool as though he were a sixteen-incher. All the fish took my dry flies seemingly without hesitation. I used a yellow jacket Humpy with white wings and the yellow-bodied Stimulator. Both were my go-to flies during my trip.

Three Roaring River beauties

Instead of cooking my trout dredged in cornmeal, I used the leftover spicy polenta. Since polenta is essentially cornmeal, the added spices gave the fish an extra special flavor. Dinner was a little sparse, aside from the fish. My food sack was running low, and I needed to pay attention to what was left.

Getting out of camp early the next morning was swift and painless. It was perhaps because I looked forward to the last day of the trip. The trail leaving Scaffold Meadow is a difficult walk. The area is *heavily* used by stock. The trail's soil has been masticated so much that what is left is fine, powdery sand. It is like walking in the sand at the beach, except much dustier.

Ferguson Creek was my next stop, and it brought back only one memory for me: my brother Scott falling off a slippery, rain-soaked log while fishing and splitting his head open on a rock. His wound took a few butterfly bandages to close, and he had to be watched constantly for a concussion. I remember spending the rest of the day lying on our sleeping bags under the tarp while it rained and hailed. It was our job to push the piles of hail off the tarp to keep the entire fly from collapsing. Mom and Dad kept Scott awake all night for fear of a concussion, worried that he may not wake up if he fell asleep. A horse packer came by the next morning and offered to take Scott and two packs (Dad's and Scott's) on horses. Scott felt fine and kept saying that he did not want to go out on horseback. Dad hiked alongside as they returned Scott on a saddle horse to the Horse Corral Pack Station. Mom followed along behind some time later and brought the rest of us kids.

I fished Ferguson Creek only to pull in one small brookie. The creek was not much more than a trickle. One pool, one cast, and one fish! What more could I ask for?

I passed Sugarloaf Creek, the site of a proud fishing moment for me in 1967. Sugarloaf Creek was where I tried catching a golden trout while wearing a red shirt. I laughed to myself, reflecting.

Fording the creek was an easy rock hop without getting my boots wet. A perfect resting spot next to the creek allowed me to ponder awhile and write in my journal. I happened to glance up into the pool in front of me. There were two small fish, maybe seven or so inches in length, lazily finning about. Every once in a while, they would swim up and take a bug off the surface. I thought for a minute that I should rig up my rod and cast a fly. Just for old time's sake! Are fish spooked by Hawaiian shirts? I wondered, amused. It might be a fashion faux pas, but I don't think fish mind all that much.

Scott's twelve-inch fish, Eric's thirteen-inch rainbow, and the author's nine-inch fish, 1967

Eric after eating his thirteen-inch rainbow, 1967

I arrived at Comanche Meadow with one memory in particular that was spurred by recognizing the area. Climbing out of the Sugarloaf area, I was leaving behind a place my family and I had visited before. Many memories flew through my head as I approached Comanche Meadow. It was here my brothers, Scott and Eric, and I amused ourselves by floating sticks down the creek during the same 1967 trip. We had stopped for a break and we could not help but play in the water. Sticks alone just weren't enough for us. We wanted more! So, we decided to use the dental floss we brought and tie the sticks together to make rafts. We spent the afternoon floating them down the creek.

I had a conversation with Dad at Florence Lake about how he and Mom never pushed us on our family trips. If us kids wanted to stop and play, that was fine with them. Dad says that, for the most part, we entertained ourselves. If we only hiked three miles that day, that was great. Being in the wilderness, together as a family, and enjoying all of it was all that mattered. Besides, he said, usually we were excited enough to get to the next camp so we could fish and explore, and it didn't take too much coaxing to keep us hiking.

From Comanche Meadow to just below the park boundary ridge, I saw that there had been another significant fire. Many standing trees were dead, and the scars indicated that at times it was a hot burn with large sections of cool, slow underburning that created a pleasant patchwork of new vegetation. It was the Williams Fire that burned in 2003. It was caused by lightning and became a managed wildfire, in all burning 3,500 acres.

The hike from Comanche Meadow to Rowell Meadow was brutal. For one, the sandy trail was difficult not only physically, but also mentally. With every step, I cursed the trail and wished for hard ground on which to step. Most of the hike was uphill, and it seemed to keep going and going.

Once I got to the park's boundary with the Sequoia National Forest, I sat and had a lunch comprised of the last few chunks of jerky—the last food item that did not need water and a fire to cook. Since I was out of water, and had not crossed a good source in a while, I decided to press on. I figured that the creek at Rowell Meadow would most likely be flowing and I could cook up some proper lunch. When I got to Rowell Meadow, the creek was dry—not a standing pool or bit of wet ground to be found.

CHAPTER 12

Return to Civilization

It was about three o'clock when I made it to the Horse Corral Pack Station. My arrival signaled the end of my backpacking trek. It was not a coincidence that I ended my trip here; it was here where, in 1945, Mom started her first trip. And, in 1967, it was where we started our family backpacking trip into the Sequoia Kings Canyon National Park on horses hired from the pack station.

As I walked into the compound, the station dog greeted me. He barked for a while until I could convince him that I was all right. No one seemed to be there, so I made myself comfortable in a chair positioned around a campfire in the center of the compound. The fire was just a smoldering heap of ashes, most likely left over from the morning's entertainment. For about thirty minutes, I enjoyed the comfort of a chair, ate some peanuts out of a big jar sitting on a stump used as a coffee table, and thumbed through an issue of *Popular Mechanics*.

Charlie Mills, the owner of the pack station, popped out of the main cabin completely unaware that anyone had been there. He was taking a nap and did not hear the dog bark, he said. We chatted for a while until I guess he was comfortable enough with me to let me use his phone to call Heidi. I left her a message when she didn't answer.

*Horse Corral Pack Station, 2012, the end of the trek
at roughly 300 miles in 33 days*

Barbara, Horse Corral Pack Station, 1945

Horse Corral Pack Station, 1945

Horse Corral Pack Station, 1967

Packer loading mules - Horse Corral to Brewer Lakes
pack trip, August 1967

Charlie and his wife have owned the station for about fourteen years. They bought it from the Simmons family, who owned it in 1967 when we packed out for our trip. The original owners were the Cecil family, who owned the station in 1945 when Mom packed out with her grandfather.

Charlie gave me a ride down to Big Meadows where there is a campground and a pay phone, a great gesture on his part and something I appreciated very much. I offered, but he declined to take any money for his troubles. I camped at the campground next to the trailhead because Charlie advised it was the closest to the payphone and next to the creek for water. When I got there, I found that the creek was dry, and was left with only the water in my water bottle to use for dinner. I gathered enough firewood for a good-sized fire and settled in for a mellow and relaxing evening.

I did not sleep much that night. There were two young guys from Germany (at least it sounded like they were speaking

German) camped next to me. They were respectful when I went to bed and were sitting around their fire, quietly drinking a few beers. That was not the issue. They retired to their tent soon after me and continued to talk until four in the morning. Not loud, just continual talk. What do two young men have to talk about while lying in a tent until four in the morning?

I was up early and wanted to get to the main highway to hitch a ride to the village. Not more than two miles down the road, the second car to pass me, a pickup belonging to a very nice older couple, stopped to give me a ride. They were heading out to fish and drove me to the highway junction where it would be just a two-mile walk to the village. I went straight to the cafe when I arrived. What a treat it was to have endless cups of hot coffee and a warm breakfast cooked by someone else.

I planned to hitchhike to Fresno and catch a bus to Santa Cruz. I was to get home that night if all went according to plan. I walked back to the highway junction and set myself up along the road. I stood there and read the entire *Fresno Bee*. The weather for Fresno was supposed to be hot and dry, with temperatures up to 105 degrees.

A young couple from Belgium on holiday finally stopped and picked me up. They were bound for Death Valley. Their route of travel was going to take them through Visalia, not Fresno, but I, not wanting to sit on the side of the highway halfway to Fresno in 105 degree heat, inquired about the possibility of them dropping me off in Visalia. They were more than willing to accommodate another hitchhiker. They told me they often hitchhike and regularly give others rides to return the favor.

We had a great visit getting to know each other and talked about some sights to see while they were in California. I suggested they visit Mono Lake, the hot springs along the Lower Kern River, Mendocino, and some other places I knew in Death Valley.

When I got to the bus depot in Visalia and bought my

ticket, I had two hours to spare. I hailed a cab and asked him to take me to the Visalia Public Cemetery. It had been many years since I was there last. Mom and Dottie, my maternal grandmother, passed away nearly two years apart. In 1991, I accompanied most of the family to the cemetery to dedicate the memorial plaque. Since it was a weekend, the office was closed, and there was no staff to assist me in finding their headstones. Going by memory, I wandered around with my backpack on in the heat of the day and finally found it: site T 21 G 33.

I miss Mom very much and wish that she were here to share my life and the lives of my kids with her. Mom had a big impact on me when I was growing up. I see it now, as an adult, because I see so much of her in me today. I know that she would be proud of her accomplishments as a mother, friend, and grandmother. She had such a special bond with my son, Justin, and I regret that she did not get to meet Brianna, her granddaughter.

Tears and a lot of reflection about her were therapeutic in some sort of way for me. I spent time with my memories and thoughts at the cemetery. The grass and weeds had invaded her headstone, so I pulled at them and cleaned the area. Dottie was also there with us, the three of us together again in spirit.

After leaving the cemetery, I caught a bus to San Jose. Following a two-hour layover, I transferred to a bus headed for Santa Cruz. A taxi ride home completed my journey in thirty-three days and over 300 trail miles.

AFTERWORD

Fishing the Waters of the Golden Trout Country: Then & Now

To quote Greek philosopher Heraclitus (c. 535 BC – 475 BC), it seems that the only constant is change. Such is true in the Sierra Nevada. In the seventy years since Mac backpacked and wrote about these golden trout waters, there has been significant change. Not only the transitions in the fisheries—the trout populations, species, and their aquatic environment—but in the visitors and the landscape of the Sierra Nevada Mountains themselves.

I spent countless hours preparing for the trip, not only organizing the equipment I would need, but reading Mac's writings, pouring over historical documents about the Sierra fisheries, and adding it all to my past and current experiences of fishing the same waters. Inherently, I tend to be inquisitive. Still, questions continue to come to mind.

I continued to stumble across one mystery after another and attempted to actively understand why the current condition exists. We have a good snapshot of past fishing conditions through the writing of Mac and others. My methods were in no way scientific, or, for that matter, complete. However, my observations are just that: my observations. So, I have attempted to answer a few questions and understand why current conditions exist.

A Change in Name

The golden trout is the official piscifaunal emblem of the State of California. It was presented to the Secretary of State on March 20, 1947, via Assembly Concurrent Resolution No. 52. The golden trout was first described in 1892 as *Salmo mykiss agua-bonita.* It was named after the Agua-Bonita waterfall at the confluence of Volcano Creek with the Kern River. In 1904, famed author Stewart Edward White wrote to his friend Theodore Roosevelt (then president) that the golden trout of California was threatened. President Roosevelt dispatched the U.S. Bureau of Fisheries and Biologist Barton Warren Evermann to study the situation. In 1906, Evermann described four forms of the fish: *Salmo roosevelti* from Golden Trout (Volcano) Creek, *Salmo aguabonita* from nearby South Fork of the Kern River, *Salmo whitei* (named in recognition of Stewart Edward White) from the Little Kern River, and *Salmo gilberti*, the Kern River rainbow.

In Mac's time, the golden trout was still called *Salmo roosevelti.* Genetic studies have since delineated the fish into three species. The California golden trout is now called *Oncorhynchus mykiss aguabonita.* It has a historical range of the South Fork of the Kern River, its tributary the Golden Trout Creek. The second is the Little Kern River golden trout (*Oncorhynchus mykiss whitei*). The last is the Kern River rainbow trout (*Oncorhynchus mykiss gilberti*).

The History of the Loch Leven Trout

Just prior to this book going to print—and, unfortunately, too late for inclusion in the main body of work—my eldest brother, Scott, sent me some details about the origin of the Loch Leven trout. Scott's naval career took him to Scotland, where he flew search and rescue missions for the British Royal Navy. Flying

helicopters to rescue stranded or injured mountaineers led him on one mission where he flew only one hundred feet above Loch Leven. He knew the area well and questioned a statement I make regarding how the Loch Leven trout got its name. In the first chapter, I state, "The lakes in that region of Scotland were simply named Loch One, Loch Two, etc. Loch Leven is the eleventh lake in the chain, thus the
name Loch Leven." This bit of information was gathered from an article I read during my research.

Scott is by far the most detailed and thoroughly researched guy I know. He questions the validity of my statement on several levels. First, being familiar with the area, he knows the lochs are not named, one, two, and so on. Three lochs in the area are in fact named, Loch Ore, Loch Gelly, and Loch Fitty. Furthermore, it is the River Leven that drains Loch Leven and travels straight to the North Sea without draining into any of the other local lochs. It may be possible that a long, long time ago, the names of the lochs were simply named Loch One, Loch Two, and so forth.

The settlement of Leven, and the loch sharing its name, has embraced that name for hundreds of years. According to Wikipedia, "The origin of the name 'Leven' comes from the Pictish word for 'flood.' The nearby Loch Leven, being the flood lake, was the name given to both the river and town." Pictish is the extinct language, or dialect, spoken by the Picts, the people of northern and central Scotland in the Early Middle Ages. It was replaced by Gaelic in the latter centuries of the Pictish period. The village of Leven has been around since at least the mid-eleventh century.

To further muddy the waters, another story is told that Leven got its name from an event where the English attempted to remove the occupants of Lochleven Castle, which is perched on an island in the lake. They attempted to flood the castle by building a dam across the outflow of the loch. The water level rose for a month until the defenders took the opportunity to come out of the castle at night and damage the dam, causing it to collapse and flood the English camp downriver. The story has, however, been doubted by historians.

Lochleven Castle has a varied history. It was once used as a prison and at one point detained Mary, Queen of Scots. In later years, after switching owners, it became a well-known vacation spot and was on several occasions visited by King Robert the Bruce. He visited the castle in 1313 and again in 1323. Then, in 1675, the Loch Leven estate was bought by Sir William Bruce (c.1630–1710), who was considered the king's royal architect in Scotland. The Bruce clan was well connected, strongly loyal to the king, and descended from Thomas Bruce, a cousin of King Robert II, son of King Robert the Bruce.

As a Bruce, I am a direct descendant of the king himself. With all that said, I am honored to say that we have a direct family tie to the castle and the loch. The fishing for brown trout in Loch Leven has historically been fit for royalty.

Interbreeding

Which Sierra trout will freely interbreed with other trout species? One ranger (Ranger Rick Sanger out of Vidette Meadow) did not think that golden trout interbred with brook trout. We had an interesting conversation when I first met him at Vidette Meadow.

There were many instances when it was clear that the fish I caught were hybrids between a golden and rainbow trout. It makes sense that the two would freely hybridize, given the fact that ichthyologists now agree that the golden trout is a subspecies of the native rainbow trout. The primary threat to the native and pure golden trout of the High Sierra is hybridization and introgression with the stocked rainbow trout.

I have not been able to find any sort of confirmation that the golden trout will hybridize with other trout species of the High Sierra. The brook trout (*Salvelinus fontinalis*), native to the east coast of the United States, is actually a char. It is known for outcompeting the golden trout for food. The brown trout (*Salmo trutta*) is known to prey on the young golden trout.

Fish Size

In the past, golden trout were moved from one watershed to another, brown trout were introduced, and rainbow trout would regularly hybridize. The big fish of yesterday appear to have given way to major populations of a single size class of fish in many lakes. Mac at one point states that he felt the big fish in one lake were dying of old age. I found lakes and sections of water containing one species of fish where, in 1945, Mac had found a completely different species.

So why did Mac catch and see so many big fish on his trips during the mid-1940s? Why was the fishing so good for Mac in 1945, with much larger, more abundant fish, compared to today? I have a few theories, although I have not been able to confirm the cause. My first, and most obvious, theory is that there is greater fishing pressure today than there was in 1945, and all the big fish have either been caught, died off, or have retreated permanently to the depths of the lakes. Another possibility is that the fish stocking programs conducted by the Department of Fish and Wildlife have somehow interfered, in some ways negatively, with today's fisheries. In the 1940s, the planting and transplanting of trout in the Sierra was limited and spotty at best. There has never been a "master plan" and there was little coordination between agencies. Moreover, fish stocking programs are themselves inherently risky as diseases are introduced, introduction of exotic organisms have occurred, and the planting of unwanted strains of fish can and have happened. All of these circumstances tend to change the fisheries in different ways.

I fished many lakes where the fish seemed to be a population of one species and one size class. Often the fish I caught were never smaller than seven inches or larger than ten inches. My theory is that the food sources available were limiting the growth of the fish and keeping them in check at one size class. My second theory, put simply, is that Mac was a much better fly fisherman and was able to catch the bigger fish.

There seems to be a much more complex answer to the above question. Although my observations may be true, I am sure that the intricate, interwoven dimensions within the fisheries all have a part to play.

Introduction of Non-Native Species

The introduction of non-native trout species appears to have had the most significant impact on the Sierra fisheries as well as other aquatic biota. The history of planting or transplanting fish into the high country has a colored and varied record. Recreational fishing seems to have been the primary goal for planting fish in the fishless lakes. Local fishing clubs, ranchers, explorers, backpackers, and official agencies, like the military and the Department of Fish and Wildlife, were all involved in moving fish from one water source to another. Other fish species that were introduced over the years included salmon, brown trout, lake trout, Dolly Varden, and the brook trout.

Mac attempted to transplant golden trout from one lake to another in the Upper Evolution Valley area. He caught several dozen six-inch golden trout from one lake behind Mount Wallace and moved them in his stewpan to another larger lake. He and Vic returned the next year to find that no fish had survived. It was, however, still swarming with polliwogs and other aquatic insects. In Mac's words, this was his transplanting attempt to "help carry on the works of the sadly undermanned Department of Fish and Game."

Close to the time of his death, in an article written for the *San Francisco Examiner & Chronicle*, staff writer Ed Neal references Mac's observation that, "the fishing has deteriorated tremendously. Heavy traffic, yes, but that has tapered off now. The introduction of spinning, which made a long range caster out of every angler, didn't help."

Stocking

Today the Department of Fish and Wildlife (whose organization name has changed as of January 1, 2013, from the Department of Fish and Game) oversees the trout stocking programs in the Sierra, their principle objectives being to maintain populations of native trout and returning waters to a "natural" condition. Stocking programs in the national parks (Yosemite, Kings Canyon, and Sequoia) were terminated in the early 1990s. However, stocking still continues in the national forests and wilderness areas to enhance recreational fishing.

Most lakes in the High Sierra contain fish. Usually those that are fishless are typically significantly smaller in size due to the fact that the habitat is unable to sustain a fish population. One might then conclude that, presently, elevation seems to not be a factor in whether a lake is fishless or not. Brook trout appear to be the most common species of trout in the Sierra Nevada, followed by rainbow, then golden, and finally brown trout. Studies have shown that some lakes (usually those that are smaller and/or at lower elevations) have lost their fish populations once the stocking programs ended. In the Yosemite, Kings Canyon, and Sequoia national parks, only twenty percent of the previously stocked lakes reverted to being fishless while the remaining eighty percent have been able to sustain a healthy fish population. Some lakes with poor spawning habitat are expected to suffer a continual decline in fish populations and may eventually revert to being fishless.

Fishlessness

Historically, before the mid 1800s, most of the lakes in the Sierra above 6,000-foot elevation were fishless. Several streams and rivers in the area were home to only two native trout species and several sub-species: the rainbow and cutthroat trout, with their sub-species, the golden trout, the Kern River rainbow, the Kern River Gilbert trout, and the Lahontan cutthroat that made their home in the low elevations of this region.

Given the number of stocking and introduction programs, I am still baffled as to why some lakes showed no sign of fish or life when others have been said to contain fish—big fish. When talking with Charlie Mills of Horse Corral Pack Station, he said that Lake South America has big fish. Yet why, during my time there, didn't I see a single fish? The Department of Fish and Game's pamphlet titled *Golden Trout of the High Sierra*, written by Leonard Fisk, has some insight on the history and distribution of the golden trout of the Sierra Nevada. The pamphlet lists waters known to or reported to contain golden trout, including Lake South America, Brown Bear Lake, Teddy Bear Lake, Silver Pass Lake, Desolation Lake, and Wanda Lake. All of these lakes, I found, appeared to be fishless and I neither caught nor saw a single fish. Granted, most of these bodies of water could use several days of exploration by an angler to truly determine if it contains a population of trout.

Frog Projects

Another activity that some land management agencies have been slowly addressing is to bring some of the High Sierra lakes back to their original condition and re-introduce some endangered species, such as the Sierra yellow-legged frog. This requires the lake to be sterilized so that all introduced fish are removed first. The frogs and their eggs are then reintroduced back into the lake without the pressures from fish in the same body of water. The predation from introduced trout has been the principle factor in the decline of frog populations. Biologists have also found a fungus that has proved lethal to the frogs and will need to be eliminated if the frog re-introduction programs are going to be successful.

There was a lot of talk regarding the frog projects among a number of the hikers that I met on the trail. One location that several hikers specifically mentioned was the Sixty Lakes Basin above the Rae Lakes. Generally, people's reaction to the project was negative, most likely because they were anglers and did not want to see their fishing grounds turned into a frog pond.

On the south side of Muir Pass, I stopped and fished the three small lakes below Lake Helen in Le Conte Canyon and did not see a single fish. I now know that these lakes are part of the frog reintroduction project. Oddly, the highest and lowest lake were devoid of life, while the middle lake was full of frogs and pollywogs. It is most likely the case that the three lakes were sterilized and the frogs and eggs were reintroduced only into the middle lake. Presumably, the frogs move around from there.

Landscape

Mac, on one trip with Vic, explained that he found Loch Leven trout in the South Fork of the San Joaquin River only as high as Blaney Meadow. He found only goldens in the river above that. Vic was perplexed and continually wondered why. Mac and Vic explored the section of river upstream from Blaney Meadow and found the mouth to a box canyon, the gorge clogged with a massive log jam. The river twists around and through a massive water-carved slice of granite with waterfalls too high for any fish to jump.

I have backpacked, fished, and explored most of the South Fork of the San Joaquin River from Florence Lake to

Evolution Creek over the years with my family. We found and enjoyed that very same log jam and gorge, seemingly unchanged for over six decades. There were fewer logs, some perhaps having been taken downstream during storms when the volume of water moving through the canyon increased, but a jam it was nonetheless. We did well, fishing the pools from atop the rocks at the edge of the gorge. There were plenty of goldens and rainbows to eleven inches and an occasional sighting of a few big fish in the sixteen- to eighteen-inch class. We just could not get the larger fish to bite.

California has been in the midst of the worst drought in decades for the last several years. Snow levels were at all-time lows and water levels were very low during my trip. The Sierra Nevada has more permanent snow and ice bodies (glaciers) than any other area in California. These snow fields have been retreating for years and many are completely diminished. Shrinkage of these glaciers are an indication of a change in the climate. Other natural and climatic influences certainly have an impact on the fishing, such as the phases of the moon, water temperatures, and weather changes. Some effects are short term and localized, while others are more broadly impacting.

Fire

Fire has certainly played a significant role in changing the landscape while at the same time keeping the natural order of the Sierra. From most visitors' point of view, the change is ugly, destructive, and a menace. The Smokey Bear campaign and its message that "Only you can prevent forest fires," has, in my opinion, been detrimental to our forests. This message, along with decades of active and aggressive fire suppression, has created an unnatural buildup of forest fuels and an unhealthy opinion of fire in our forests. What would normally be naturally occurring, smaller, low-intensity fires are now larger, high-intensity fires that are devastating to the environment. Most people today identify forest fires as a bad thing and cannot differentiate the benefits between a natural fire and man-caused fire. People see black and burned trees, soil that has been denuded and spalted, and vegetation that is struggling to take hold. Fire management specialists now know that fire is needed and often required for many plant species to survive. Much of the Sierra Nevada vegetation evolved because of fire. It is a natural component of a healthy forest ecosystem. It is actually this "change" that struggles to maintain consistency. Without fire, there would certainly be a change or shift in vegetation types to an unnatural state within these mountains.

Natural fire tends to have little impact on the fisheries and watersheds of the High Sierra. A larger unnatural fire near a stream or river in the riparian zone may have a short-term impact by slightly increasing water temperatures or siltation. These factors tend to have an influence on spawning habitat of Sierra trout.

Grazing

Mac commented about seeing grazing sheep. I went my entire trip without seeing any cattle or sheep until I approached Horse Coral Meadow. Grazing is still allowed in parts of the National Forest and in many areas there is a huge impact on the environment. Grazing in the national parks was discontinued in the early 1990s and the meadows are better off for it.

Fortunately, most of the High Sierra has been untouched by manmade landscape changes. Over the years, man has influenced the environment and fisheries by overgrazing of animals like sheep, cattle, and stock horses. The presence of grazing animals in the creeks and meadows damages riparian habitat and creates an unnatural impact on the aquatic environment. New conservation measures are in place and appear to be having a positive impact.

Today's Fisheries

When early explorers first arrived in the High Sierra, the fisheries were in a much different state than they are today. The scientific community undoubtedly knows much more about the influences and health of the High Sierra fisheries and habitat than they knew seventy years ago. Transplantation and introduction of new fish species to these waters has had a tremendous impact. Aquatic ecosystems in the Sierra Nevada show that introduced trout can have severe impacts on native trout, amphibians, and zooplankton. The food web of these alpine ecosystems tends to be narrow and fragile, something that allows for significant changes in a relatively short period of time. Interbreeding, predation, and increasing fishing pressure have all taken their toll, each contributing factors to the changing Sierra fishery.

From my perspective, the fishing was fantastic over the duration of my trek. Each day I fished and explored some of the most beautiful and picturesque bits of water. I didn't always catch fish; however, most days I landed more fish than I could count. They may not have been big fish, but I caught fish nonetheless. For me, a good fishing experience also includes just being near the water, with no one in sight, enjoying such a beautiful area. The largest fish I caught was fifteen inches—much smaller than what Mac was catching during his trips into the Sierra—although I did have an encounter with a much larger fish in Thousand Island Lake. This is a hopeful sign that the fisheries could still be healthy and there exists environments that will harbor populations of big fish.

On several occasions, I traversed cross country to lakes and fishable water that sees very little fishing pressure. Often I was rewarded with an incredible experience, take Lake 10296 for example. At other times, I was met with waters that appeared to be fishless. I am still amazed at the unpredictability of the fisheries of the out-of-the-way locations. You never know what lies below the water's surface. This brings to mind the lunker at Thousand Island Lake again, or the brown trout at Roaring River. You expect one thing (based on word of mouth, guide books, past experience, or the first few fish you catch), and then *wham!* A curve ball is thrown at you. I love the excitement associated with arriving at one of these fishing spots.

I did notice that the overall size of the fish I caught were much smaller than the fish from Mac's days. This leads me to believe that the fisheries are in fact declining, at least in the sense of fish size. From strictly a comparison standpoint, my fishing experience was much different than Mac's and my great-grandfather's. By any angler's standards, the fishing in the Sierra is evidently rewarding, and the angler can catch numerous trout of multiple species in a wide variety of fishable waters. Yet I can't help but wonder how the fishing used to be if we see such a seemingly stable and healthy fishery but recognize that increasing fishing pressure, environmental factors, and the work of the land management agencies is gradually altering it.

Let's Talk Water

The only time in my life that I treated or filtered my water while backpacking was with my son and daughter, Justin and Brianna, when they were young. I had made a promise to their mother that I would do so, and even then I only filtered *their* water.

By conscious decision, this trip was no different. I chose to backpack without filtering or treating my water for the entire trip. I did bring, but never used, a few "emergency" iodine pills. My good friend and former paramedic, Adam, and his wife gave me a SteriPEN to use on my trip. I was grateful and accepted this generous gift. I think he was little "bent" when, after I returned, I told him that I left it behind with Heidi and chose not to treat my water.

Today, backcountry visitors are told not to consume untreated water. Land management agencies are constantly instilling the fear that if untreated water is consumed, the visitor will get giardiasis, caused by the flagellated protozoan *Giardia lamblia*. *Giardia lamblia* attaches itself to the lining of the digestive tract of its host. It can potentially produce over one billion offspring in just fifteen days that are distributed from the host through defecation in the form of a cyst. The cysts can live in cold water for up to three months, but cannot tolerate and will eventually die in freezing (winter) conditions, thus any contamination must begin again each spring. The cysts are transported only three ways, through contaminated water, contaminated food, and direct fecal-oral routes. Giardiasis is the disease caused by ingesting the protozoan *Giardia lamblia*. Symptoms of this disease (usually including diarrhea, loose or watery stools, and stomach cramps) will usually appear in one to two weeks after ingestion of cysts. However, some hosts may be completely asystematic of the usual symptoms.

It is my theory and belief that *Giardia* is not as prevalent in the Sierra as it is thought to be and that our public land management agencies (e.g., the US Forest Service, the National Park Service, and the Bureau of Land Management) have gone overboard in leading us to believe that it is a major issue. To protect its visitors from *Giardia*, they suggest that all water needs to be treated before consumed. I am convinced that their relentless water treatment campaigns are solely based upon liability reasons and have little to no science to back their claims. To go further, I don't know of anyone that can definitely say that they ingested the *Giardia* protozoa from drinking untreated water in the Sierra. What's more, I have never contracted giardiasis from drinking the water straight from the source while backpacking in the Sierra, the Appalachians, or the Rockies.

Now, maybe there are other reasons as to why I have not contracted giardiasis. Perhaps I have simply been lucky to have not ingested enough cysts to cause the disease. It could be the case that I have an abnormally insensitive gut that can digest just about anything without issue. Or, the simple explanation is that

Giardia lamblia is rare in the Sierra.

Upon my return, I did some extensive research on the subject. Although the issue is still shrouded in much controversy, there have been numerous scientific studies that have been published that demonstrate the accuracy of my theories, if only my last theory that *Giardia lamblia* is rare in the Sierra. One of the most respected and cited source comes from Dr. Robert L. Rockwell, PhD, titled *Giardia Lamblia and Giardiasis with Particular Attention to the Sierra Nevada.* Dr. Rockwell states that his information is the "result of a critical distillation of relevant articles, retaining only those from scholarly, peer-reviewed, or otherwise professional and trustworthy sources." Dr. Rockwell's publication has to be the most direct and applicable scientific literature I have found on the subject.

In conclusion, Dr. Rockwell states that proper personal hygiene is far more important in avoiding giardiasis than treating the water in the Sierra. His research concludes that an individual's diarrheal symptoms (the most common and severe of the symptoms) may very well be that of a different organism. He believes that of those who do contract giardiasis while in the Sierra, it is not from drinking hazardous water. Some wild animals, including beaver, coyotes, deer, elk, and squirrels, are known to carry *Giardia*. Domestic cattle can also carry *Giardia*, however horses and domestic sheep, apparently, are not hosts for the parasite.

Giardia appears to have always been in the Sierra Nevada watershed, but I believe that it is not in a high enough concentration to be of any concern. Drink wisely and practice good hygiene while cooking and preparing food. Dr. Rockwell believes that if you get diarrheal symptoms while in the backcountry, it will go away and you will most likely be better off since you are building up an immunity to the organism that may have contributed to the symptoms. Dr. Rockwell further suggests that hikers be smart about the water they drink and follow these suggestions. Spring water is filtered by the soil and should be safe. Colder water is usually less contaminated than warmer water. Water upstream from a trail crossing or high use area is usually safer to drink than the water downstream from those areas. Water at higher elevations is usually less contaminated than water at lower elevations. It is also safer to drink clear, not cloudy, water. Studies have also found that moving water may contain fewer Giardia cysts than still water. Drink smart.

Through-Hikers, Ultra-Lights & Baggers:
The Human Species of the Sierra High Country

It never fails to amaze or entertain me to stop and talk to the John Muir and Pacific Crest Trail through-hikers. They are a varied bunch of people. Some are hardcore from start to finish, refusing to miss or skip a section or even a ten-foot stretch of trail. Most used trekking poles. Towner described them as looking like spiders walking down the trail. Many were ultra-light trekkers, wearing running shoes and small backpacks. One solo hiker I talked to was using his poncho as his only shelter. Some were run-of-the-mill backpackers out to enjoy the entire experience, while others were section hikers enjoying their trek in small doses, anticipating the trip in the coming year so they could hike the next section. Most did not fish and those that did were sure to ask how I found the fishing to be.

I use the term "bagger" to describe some of these ultra-light hikers. The term is usually reserved for someone that sets out to reach the highest points of a number of collective peaks, i.e., the twelve fourteeners in California. I have adapted the meaning of this term to describe the numerous through-hikers that attempt to complete the hike as fast as they possibly can. These individuals boast about their daily mileage and their least number of days to complete it, and are so focused on the goal that they usually fail to enjoy the trek. It seems to diminish the adventure for the primary purpose of obtaining their goals of climbing to the tops of mountains in the least amount of time. These people are obsessive to the point that enjoying the backcountry and scenery is severely reduced in significance or is lost.

Then there was me. I did not want to be associated with the John Muir Trail crowd. I was on a different quest, and when asked, I always presented myself as such so as not to be lumped into the through-hiker crowd, just to make me feel better about my purpose.

As a youngster backpacking in these mountains, I remember seeing very few people on the trails. Now, I equate hiking the John Muir Trail to driving on Interstate 405 through Los Angeles—there's traffic at any time of the day. The Rae Lakes and North Lake to South Lake Loops are similar to being on Highway 17 over the Santa Cruz Mountains, busy at times, only a few passing cars at other times. The High Sierra Trail is comparable to a country road, a passing car every few hours. And yet every time I ventured off any main trail, I found the backcountry as it should be: quiet and wild with not a soul around for miles.

Technology? In the Backcountry?

It was amazing to me that people in the backcountry could not leave behind their electronic gadgets. Kevin, a businessman from Oregon, had his iPhone with him and kept checking and responding to emails to close a business deal while at Reds Meadow. One John Muir Trail "bagger," doing an average of twenty-seven miles a day, had a GPS, iPod, and solar panel to recharge his devices, all hooked up as he was hiking near the Red Cones.

As I was coming down Islands Pass toward Thousand Island Lake, I had one fly rod rigged up in my hand and the other in the soft case attached to my pack. As I approached a hiker on the trail, the hiker said, "You have an antenna!" My response was, jokingly, "Yes, I am looking for cell phone coverage." His reply to my remark was matter-of-fact as he exclaimed, "Oh! If you go up to Lake Cecile, you can get a clear shot to the cell tower on top of Mammoth Mountain." I was so dumbfounded that I didn't have the heart to tell him that the antenna-like protrusion from my pack was just a fishing pole. I simply thanked him as we parted. After a few moments, I thought of the perfect reply to his initial statement. I should have told him that I worked for a new division of Google called Google Trails and that I was mapping all the trails in the area. What would his reply have been then?

Another instance of technology's presence in the backcountry occurred while coming down Le Conte Canyon near its upper reaches. I came across two guys lying against their packs, resting right on the trail's edge. They were heading south and had given up for the day. One guy was reading a book and the other was reading his Kindle Fire!

The Return Home

While riding a Greyhound bus from Visalia to San Jose on my return home, I had the opportunity to reflect on a lot of memories and thoughts about my journey, previous family backpack trips, fishing, and myself.

I remember a particular backpack trip I took with Justin and Dad to the Gold Lakes area in Northern California. Upon our return, eight-year-old Justin had a surprising answer to his mom's question. When asked how the trip was, Justin replied, "Great, except Papa made me eat fish for breakfast. I don't like fish for breakfast."

Every trip into the wilderness affects me in some way. I learned a thing or two from my trip. For one, next time I will take a bigger and more powerful headlamp. I tended to do my journaling in the evening just before I went to bed. A stronger headlamp would have helped. Secondly, I am not much of a photographer. My camera is simple and easy to use. I only brought one battery, never thinking that two would be needed. Two camera batteries are a must. I missed many perfect opportunities to capture the ideal shot because my battery ran dead. Oddly, I took a sketch pad and never had time to use it. I really thought that I would have lots of down time to sit and sketch. For future trips, I will either make time to sketch or leave the sketchpad behind to avoid lugging around the added weight. Lastly, although I enjoyed hiking alone, I missed being with my family, especially in the evenings around the campfire. Not being able to share the joys and experiences of the day was very much missed. I would prefer to backpack with my family, but would jump at the opportunity to embark on another extended solo trip.

On this particular journey, I realized what makes for a good fishing experience: my ability to reach an inner calmness. A good experience is the feeling of being on the water, my heart rate dropping, my mind relaxing and focusing on the task at hand, and my senses finely tuning into my surroundings: the sounds of the water, the wind through the trees, the bird's song in the distance. A good fishing adventure, for me, is not about how many fish I catch or if I catch big fish.

What constitutes a good backcountry experience, in my opinion, is fishing for thirty-three days straight and being enticed by the continual mystery of what lies under the water. For over a month, I was able to explore fishing waters unimpeded by outside influences, something that proves to be central to my ideal Sierra fishing adventure.

In the end, I was left wanting more. I constantly found myself staring up into the rocks upriver or the rushing water downriver and yearning for what they had to offer. I made mental notes along the way of the places where I will return so I can continue my explorations of the High Sierra waters.

AUTHOR'S NOTE

Who Was Charles K. McDermand?

When I started my research for this trip, I became interested in wanting to know whom Charles McDermand was. Information, I found, was slim and I realized that I had to do a lot of digging. What was he like? Does he have family members or relatives that are still living? What was his fishing and backpacking background? Where did he grow up and what were his early days like? I felt compelled to get to know who he was so that I may better understand some of the relationships between this fisherman, the fish he sought, his hiking buddies, and the High Sierra.

Charles Kenneth McDermand was a relatively unknown man that unwittingly, I am sure, produced a cult-like following though his writing. He was known as "Kenny" by his family, "Mac" by his fishermen friends, and "Charlie" to his work colleagues. Some just called him Charles. He was born on February 13, 1902, to E.T. "Ted" McDermand and Lula Valetta Venters (b. 1878 – d. 1968). They were a homesteading family in Billings, Montana, where Mac had easy access to the outdoors.

Mac graduated from Montana State University with a degree in Forestry. Some time later, during the depression, he arrived in San Francisco to look for work and became interested in fishing for steelhead on the Klamath River. While working at the Emporium (Sears Emporium's old Cabin Sports Shop), they would not give him time off to fish so every July he would quit his job and go fish the Klamath River until the snow started to fall. He would then return to get rehired at his old job.

Mac, left, and hiking partner Vic

He began to write shortly after and submitted numerous pieces to various magazines and had several articles published in *Field & Stream, Outdoor Life, National Sportsman, Pacific Sportsman,* and *Fur-Fish-Game.* It was from these articles that Mac brought forth the success of his first book, *The Waters of the Golden Trout Country.* Mac's second book, *Yosemite and Kings Canyon Trout,* was published in 1947. It is another wonderful read, telling stories about fishing and hunting those areas while on several trips. Later in 1960, Mac wrote a chapter titled "Sierra Trout" for his friend and fellow author Joseph Wampler in *High Sierra Wonderland.*

By this time, Mac had quite a following. So much so, years after writing his books, he complained, "They sent too many people scurrying into the Sierra to sample what I'd done the hard way." (Ed Neal, *San Francisco Sunday Examiner & Chronicle*, December 10, 1967)

In the *San Diego Union,* a staff writer with the initials of RW on an unknown date described McDermand as "a glittering phrase-maker without peer, a fly fisherman of substance, a teacher, a pioneer of wilderness backpacking who dozens of times hiked his way along the 186-mile John Muir Trail surmounting the crest of California's Sierra Nevada." He was also said to be "the first to put it all down on paper, how to survive the mountain sanctuary of the goldens."

Mac's last job was that of a business representative for the Department Store Employees Union Local 1100 in San Francisco. He married his wife, Helen, and had two sons, Edwin and Mark. I was unable to locate any living relatives of McDermand's. Interestingly, on or about October 16, 1980, Mark McDermand murdered his mentally ill brother, Edwin, and sleeping seventy-four-year-old Helen. He was arrested and sentenced to life in prison at San Quentin State Prison and was at one time the prime suspect in the trailside killings of Marin County. Mark died in prison.

Charles K. McDermand died on December 27, 1966, of a stroke. His ashes were scattered over the Sierra by plane.

References

Alsup, William. *Missing in the Minarets: The Search for Walter A. Starr, Jr.* El Portal, CA: The Yosemite Association, 2001. Print

Beck, Steve. *Trout Fishing the John Muir Trail.* Portland, Oregon: Frank Amato Publications, Inc., 2000. Print.

Blehm, Eric. *The Last Season.* New York: Harper Perennial, 2006. Print

Farquhar, Francis P. *History of the Sierra Nevada.* Berkeley, CA: University of California Press, 1965. Print.

Fisk, L, 1988, *Golden Trout of the High Sierra,* State of California Department of Fish and Game, Sacramento, CA.

McDermand, Charles K. *Yosemite and Kings Canyon Trout.* New York, NY: G.P. Putnam's Sons, 1947. Print.

McDermand, Charles K. *Waters of the Golden Trout Country.* New York, NY: G.P. Putnam's Sons, 1946.

Neal, Ed. "A Memorial to McDermand." *San Francisco Sunday Examiner & Chronicle* [San Francisco] 8 January 1967: Page 4. Print.

Neal, Ed. "Death Takes Angling Pal." *San Francisco Examiner [San Francisco]* 28 December 1966: Page 50. Print.

Neal, Ed. "Local Angler is Honored." *San Francisco Sunday Examiner & Chronicle* [San Francisco] 10 December 1967: Page 10. Print.

R.W. *San Diego Union* [San Diego] Unknown date. Print.

Starr, Jr., Walter A. *Guide to the John Muir Trail and High Sierra Region.* San Francisco, CA: The Sierra Club, 1964. Print.

Storer, Tracey and Robert Usinger. *Sierra Nevada Natural History: An Illustrated Handbook.* Berkeley, CA: University of California Press, 1963. Print.

Van Zant, George. "Brown Trout of the Eastern Sierra." Big Fish Tackle, 25 September 2008. Web. 11 February 2015. <http://www.bigfishtackle.com/fishing_articles/Featured_Fishi ng_Authors/George_Van_Zant/Jed_Welsh_- _Brown_Trout_of_the_Eastern_Sierra_338.html>.

Wales, J. H. *Trout of California.* Sacramento, CA: State of California Department of Fish and Game, 1957. Print.

Wampler, Joseph, Weldon F. Heald, and Charles K. McDermand. *High Sierra Mountain Wonderland.* Berkely, CA: Joseph Wampler, 1960. Print.

Wikimedia Foundation, Inc. "Leven, Fife." Wikipedia, 19 July 2014. Web. February 12 2015. <http://en.wikipedia.org/wiki/Leven,_Fife>.

ABOUT THE AUTHOR

As an experienced backpacker and outdoorsman, author Todd Bruce has cultivated a deep knowledge and endless love of the natural world. Starting at age four with a fly rod in his hand, his life lessons progressed through the teachings of his family and mentors, and eventually he achieved the rank of Eagle Scout.

His passion for the outdoors led him to pursue a degree in forestry at Humboldt State University. His thirty-two year career as a firefighter began with fighting wildfires for the United States Forest Service. In 2011, he retired at the rank of captain from Santa Clara County Fire Department.

He continues to chronicle his expeditions and share his mastery of the backcountry. Bruce currently lives in Santa Cruz, California.

A Note about the Back Cover Photograph

This picture is a combination of two pictures that my son JT painstakingly merged. When I arrived at the top of Colby Pass on the second to last day of my journey, I noticed the sharp angular rock that was on the right side of the Goldman group picture. I wanted to get a picture of me in front of the very same rock, on the same pass, with over sixty-seven years stretching between them. Since I did not have a copy of the photo at the time, I had to go by memory. The photo was still in slide form and was in the slide rack from my mother's family photo collection.

When I returned from my trip and had a chance to view the two pictures side by side, it was then I realized that I had inadvertently stood on the opposite side of the rock from my mother and the Goldman group. I'm glad I did. My stepdaughter Jade had the suggestion to bring the two photos together and JT made it happen. There can be, in my opinion, no finer representation of past and present in the High Sierra than this photograph.

Made in the USA
Las Vegas, NV
07 August 2022

52860217R00135